# CHOICES

*Best Wishes,*

*[signature]*

# CHOICES

My Journey After Leaving
My Husband for Martina
and a Lesbian Life

## Judy Hill Nelson

A BIRCH LANE PRESS BOOK
Published by Carol Publishing Group

A Birch Lane Press Book

Published by Carol Publishing Group
Birch Lane Press is a registered trademark of Carol Communications,
    Inc.
Editorial Offices: 600 Madison Avenue, New York, N.Y. 10022
Sales and Distribution Offices: 120 Enterprise Avenue, Secaucus,
    N.J. 07094
In Canada: Canadian Manda Group, One Atlantic Avenue, Suite 105,
    Toronto, Ontario M6K 3E7
Queries regarding rights and permissions should be addressed to
Carol Publishing Group, 600 Madison Avenue, New York, N.Y. 10022

Carol Publishing Group books are available at special discounts for
bulk purchases, sales promotion, fund-raising, or educational
purposes. Special editions can be created to specifications. For
details, contact: Special Sales Department, Carol Publishing Group,
120 Enterprise Avenue, Secaucus, N.J. 07094

Manufactured in the United States of America
10  9  8  7  6  5  4  3  2  1

Library of Congress Cataloging-in-Publication Data
Nelson, Judy.
    Choices : my journey after leaving my husband for Martina and a lesbian life / Judy
Hill Nelson ; foreword by Pepper Schwartz.
        p.  cm.
    "A Birch Lane Press book."
    ISBN 1-55972-328-9
        1. Nelson, Judy.    2. Navratilova, Martina, 1956–    .    3. Lesbians—
    United States—Biography.    4. Coming out (Sexual orientation)—
    United States—Case studies.    I. Title.
    HQ75.4.N45A3    1996
306.76'63'092—dc20
[B]                                                                                              95-26397
                                                                                                      CIP

*To Kay*

Please keep in mind that I do not pretend to be a historian or a therapist, or an authority on moral issues. I merely give my thoughts from my own perspectives and tell my story as I have lived it. If my experiences offer any insights at all, then I am thankful.

Even in telling my story, I have done so with much trepidation. Consistent with my Southern upbringing, I have tried not to offend anyone. Just in case I have, I ask your forgiveness.

# CONTENTS

# FOREWORD

This is a book about life. About how surprising it is, how demanding and painful it can be, and how ultimately rewarding it is, even if we stagger under its revelations and challenges.

Judy Nelson has written the most personal and naked of autobiographies. And while it might seem as if its most compelling theme would be the transition of a heterosexual American beauty queen into the high-profile lover of Martina Navratilova and Rita Mae Brown, I think its most moving message is about the journey to adulthood for women. About how to find yourself, about learning to bestow love on yourself as well as on others—and how to enjoy life even when it delivers you some enormous blows.

Finding one's own way is not an easy thing for women who were born before the 1960s. After all, most women of Judy's generation, and my own, were assiduously taught how to be less than grown-up—if being grown-up meant being yourself, being self-sufficient, and picking out a life that pleased you rather than existing for other people's desires. We were taught, by people who were trying to pass on what their parents had passed on to them, that there was only one way to be a worthy woman. We were told that if we played our parts very well, if we were a household saint, an endlessly talented mother, companion, and playmate, not to mention sex goddess—if we were very, very good—we would find our prince and he would take care of us for ever and ever.

I don't think I have to remind many people of current divorce statistics to tell us that lots of women were wrong. Divorce is not an uncommon part of many women's journey to self-knowledge and self-sufficiency. However, Judy's coming of age involved a more complex passage. She found out that fairy tales are just that. And that even if you change the gender of the players, not everything works out happily ever after. It turns out that princesses, as well as princes, are pretty darn unreliable. After Judy discarded a lifetime's socialization to find her true love, a woman, she lost her. After she had endured the scandal of the relationship, after she had convinced her family to support her and create a new extended family, and after she had learned about life on the road with a superstar, she had to endure rejection on a grand scale. She became everyone's favorite villain when she dared to consider her seven-year relationship a marriage, her breakup a divorce, and her losses something that should be compensated. Finally, she had to leave a wifely self-image, both in heterosexual and homosexual marriage, and find a way to be her own person and not a handmaiden to either a man's or woman's endless ego. She had to know who were true friends and who were not. She learned the meaning of perfidy and betrayal when unscrupulous "investors" bilked her out of most of the money she had in the world.

How do you come out of this kind of past still sunny, excited about the future, ready to love again, and able to do it with a free and open heart? It is not easy, but she does. And the way she does it is through nature, sports, time alone, friendships, and by digging deep back into her roots and family. These last two, family and friends, are critically important. While some friends desert her, presumably to stay in good standing with the much more powerful and famous Martina, other friendships prove fast and are what give her the courage to continue her suit and enjoy life again. Imagine, the press of the *world* is calling you every dirty name there is, but some people stand by you. Judy's book is continually about these kind of friends—the kind of friends you make over a lifetime, and who sometimes get the chance to prove what they are made of and what they are worth.

Even more, this is a book about family: the family you grow up in, the family you make, the family that chooses you. One of the reasons Judy is such a sweet person must surely be these darling grandparents and parents of hers—the whole kit and caboodle that stand by Judy, no matter whether or not they can fathom her choices. It must be this family that has given her extraordinary capacity for love, for forgiveness, for trusting her heart. It must be these people who have allowed Judy to keep her capacity for love even when it has not been honored.

Judy's sons and parents seem never to have wavered from their love and support for her. Sure, they tried to convince her to follow the traditional heterosexual guidelines they have followed all their lives. But still, when all is said and done, they take Martina in and treat the two women as if they were a conventional couple. They cook, they clean, they are a traveling fan club and support staff. They remind us how brilliant a jewel a loving family is—how irreplaceable their positive regard and support. She reminds us to cherish them, to consider them part of life after marriage—to know, no matter what, that a tight family's love really is inviolate and continuing.

This is a book, in fact, that is eloquent and thoughtful about love. This is one of the few books I've ever read where someone really lets you know the full extent of the consequences of choices that didn't work out. Judy's sons let us know how the breakup of Judy's relationship affected their lives. And they show what children can do for parents when parents are needy.

Judy faced a firestorm of public outrage when she asked for what she reasonably felt was economic justice. But instead of backing away, she fought. And going up against a famous, rich, and powerful former partner is not a matter for the weak of heart. She never asks for our respect or affection. Yet she earns it because it is not hard to tell how difficult it has been for her. Despite the glitzy aspects of her life with Martina, she has had to face the prospect of being broke, jobless, callously rejected, and in addition to all this, castigated when she acted on the belief she thought others would share with her: that there is a bargain in a traditional marriage that must be honored. If she was to give up her personal freedom to be the companion of a breadwinner, whatever the gender, then surely her partner—who in this case could well afford to honor her previous agreement—would feel as she did that the relationship merited a fair division of finances. What was always fascinating about the Judy-Martina breakup was that it was liberals and gay people, as well as conservatives, who condemned Judy for asking for money from Martina. The very people who were least likely to be homophobic did not truly see the relationship as a marriage where the sacrifices of one person to the other's career are recognized by some equitable division of finances when the relationship ends.

Judy bravely, and I do mean bravely, shows other women, of any stripe relationship, how hard it is to get justice—but how good it is for one's self-esteem to try. And she also shows how important it is to evolve a set of values: for yourself about how you want to be treated, about how dependent you should allow yourself to be, but also a larger social hypothesis—values about lifestyle and politics. She realizes, as we all do, that finding someone who loves you for yourself can only happen if you love yourself well enough to protect the integrity of your person—in love or outside of it.

Judy's journey seems like a voyage in search of her sexual and emotional center, and to some extent it is. But to me, it is about learning to be a *real* grown-up—to learn that the only one who will really take care of you, and your children, is likely to be *you*. And that is the working hypothesis that every women has to have. She finds, like women all over the world, that the definition of a joint household, of commitment itself, breaks down when valuable goods are at stake. Her love affairs with high-visibility (and high-maintenance) lovers are familiar, except that usually the person who doesn't want to share, but who wants continuing and total service, who has the big and un-generous ego, is male.

The message of this book, however, should not be confused by the gender of the players. This book shows how to see one-self more clearly, to follow one's deepest and dearest instincts, to take responsibility for one's acts, and to understand being loved and being a lover. It shows how to recover from bad de-cisions and to love life even when life is hard. And it shows us that there can, eventually, be a better day. A pretty good thing for all of us to learn.

—Pepper Schwartz
Professor, University of Washington

# PREFACE

I realize now that my life is made up of the sum total of my choices. This book is my reflection on those choices and how they have affected my life. It is this reflection that has brought me full circle to the person I think of today as just plain Judy.

My great hope is that in telling my story I can help bridge the gap just a little more between homosexuals and heterosexuals. I hope that readers will come to realize how little difference there is between the structure of a gay or lesbian relationship and a heterosexual one.

I hope also to speak out positively about the importance of commitment in relationships, with honesty and forthrightness at their core.

I hope to demonstrate that family values are important in all relationships and that parenting is not exclusive to heterosexuals.

I hope to speak to that voice in all of us that cries out for the freedom to be ourselves.

I want to continue to emphasize the importance of women being taught to believe and to know that we can take care of ourselves.

I hope that by putting my story out there for all to see and read that other women, no matter what age, will realize that they are not alone in their journey to find their own identity, whatever it may be.

# ACKNOWLEDGMENTS

To Eddie and Bales for sharing with me the joys and tears of all my choices.

To my mom and dad, brother and sister, for always being courageous, loving, and supportive. You have taught me through your example what sacrifice really means. I want also to recognize my aunts, uncles, nieces, nephews, and cousins for your acceptance of my choices. You have all added to the richness of my life's experiences.

To Judy Twersky for always believing in me and being the best public relations agent anyone could ever have.

To Allan Wilson, my editor at Carol Publishing Group, who believed that I could write this book and believed that it was a story worth telling.

To Dr. Sharon Beckman Brindley, my therapist in Charlottesville, for teaching me how to be still.

To Martina for giving me the courage to change my life.

To Rita Mae for suggesting that I tell this story and insisting that I needed the discipline.

And to Kay for inspiring and supporting me in this endeavor; for believing I could do it; for burning the late-night oil (literally), while editing and correcting my grammar; for knowing my flaws and loving me anyway; and for all the mornings and all the nights since first we met. I love you.

## TO MY FRIENDS

To Debbie Morris for helping me through the days of despair and pain. She gave me the silence and beauty of the snowy mountains in Aspen. She showed me calm. She let me cry. She offered me peace when I had none. The peace was within her and she shared it. She was a wonderful ski instructor and she took me almost every day to the top of the mountain and taught me to listen to the silence. She taught me how to mend my soul.

To Sandra Faulkner, the coauthor of my first book *Love Match*, for giving me her unfailing support. Her insights have helped me understand my situation more clearly. Her gentleness has calmed me. She is also my rock.

To Patricia Ryan for teaching me more than anyone else about the lesbian lifestyle that I have chosen. She helped me understand the issues at hand when I had never really taken the time to examine them. She helped encourage me to have a voice, my own voice, and speak out for the causes in which I believed. She trusted and believed in me when others in the gay and lesbian community doubted my integrity.

To Carolyn Maki, who is one of those people who is admired for her willingness to just be herself—no pretenses. She is an example of the kind of person I would like to be more like. She just "lays it on the line" and you always know exactly where you stand. I watch her and I learn from her. I respect her.

To the Beegles, who have become my second family. Their home has become my home away from home. I admire the rapport they share with each other and with their friends. They are truly the most giving people that I have ever met. I was alone in Virginia. I needed a family. Mine were all back in Texas. The Beegles took me in as one of theirs. They reinforce my sense of unity and family values. They give me unconditional love.

To Travis Critzer, who is one of the important men in my life. He is married to his lovely wife, Angie, and has two young sons, Trey and Josh. Travis has a simple kind of wisdom far beyond his youthful years. I watch him and remember what truth and honor really mean. I remember what hard work can accomplish. I remember what devotion to one's family can mean. There is love in his heart for his family that is bigger than Texas. He has never judged my life choices. He has helped me, often before he helped himself. He is young in years but old in his wisdom.

To Dr. Michael Iott, who is another important man in my life. He's the kind of guy you want to introduce to all your closest friends because you want to share with them treasures in life that you have found. Michael is my treasure. He has stayed with me through thick and thin. He has held a mirror up to my face and challenged me to have a good look. Look I did. From that I have grown. He taught me to be kinder to myself.

To Annie Denver, Jane Moy, Julie Anthony, and Gigi Fernandez for remaining an important part of my life. It would have been easier for them to look the other way. For their courage and the joy of their friendship I am eternally grateful.

To Kim for being a true friend and an unbiased critic.

To Joyce Shöffner for taking the loveliest photos and making me look far better than I am.

To Trish Faulkner, who has been a true friend since the day we met. Her creativeness and unequaled work ethic have encouraged me to move forward when I had no hope. She has always been a source of inspiration to me. I cherish her.

To Dianah Barton Branum, who has remained my faithful friend since high school, never questioning my intent or my integrity.

To Dianne Hardin Sztamenits, who has been my friend since we were five years old. Although we rarely see each other, we know each other's heart.

To Marilyn Graham, who is, and has been since we met, the best friend I could ever hope to have. She has brought joy and laughter into my life far beyond what my words can ever say. We share an unspoken bond of admiration and loyalty.

To BeAnn Sizemore, who was my touchstone during my

years with Martina. She was my pulse. She helped me focus on what was real and helped me to separate it from fantasy.

To Jay Skaggs, who is a most sensitive, loyal, and compassionate friend. She has given so much of her time and talent to me. She is a shining example of womanhood in my life.

To Susan Spears Miller, who to me represents the epitome of motherhood and who will always have a very special place in my heart. A more faithful friend cannot be found.

To Jerry Loftin, my attorney, but more importantly my friend. He always shares his laughter with me. He is pure gold.

To Jane Greenawalt, a true lady. She has touched my soul. She has shared my joy and my pain. There are few greater gifts than this. I am blessed.

To Patty Sicular, my wonderful booking agent at the Ford Modeling Agency, who had confidence enough in me to sign me to a contract with such a prestigious agency. I am both grateful and flattered.

In memory of Joy Garrett, my special friend, who in her short lifetime touched many lives through her acting and singing career. Just remembering her voice will forever bring a song to my heart.

Certainly there are other very special friends in my life, and they will find themselves amongst the pages of this book.

# INTRODUCTION

# A Profound Revelation
# of a Good Southern Woman

In the middle of the night, startled, I sat straight up in my bed, beads of sweat caressing my forehead. The dream was recalled vividly as I replayed it like a movie in my mind. From that very moment I was more clear about the purpose of my life than ever before. It was truly the most profound dream that I had ever had.

In the dream I was sitting calmly on the edge of my mother's bed having a conversation with her about what I felt was the purpose of my life—the lessons I had been taught along the way and the extraordinary choices I had made in order to learn them. According to my dream (and I had never before consciously had this thought), one part of my life's purpose was to help my own family—not only my immediate family but also my grandparents, aunts, uncles, cousins, nieces, nephews, my own children and all of their children and grandchildren to come—to overcome their prejudices about a way of life they could simply not comprehend: that of being a homosexual.

They were never uncompassionate with their views of the

gay and lesbian lifestyle, nor did they stand in judgment. Usually the message was that they felt "sorry" for gays. Some even believed that it was an illness that one caught somehow, for which one could call the doctor for a cure. Or that if given love and guidance, one could simply make a choice to come "back" into the realm of a "normal" and healthy lifestyle—that of a heterosexual.

It was and has been my example, my free choice to love and live with a woman, that changed all that prejudice within my family forever. Neither they nor I will ever be the same.

I was born and bred to be a good Southern woman, the definition of which has remained constant for generations. The operative word being *good*. And that I was. Even today, it is the one word that causes me the most anxiety—for when I fall short of that expectation, I still feel great guilt. *Guilt* being a word I hate and will spend my life trying to erase from my vocabulary. (I have eradicated the word *sin*, so there is hope!)

However, at age thirty-eight I fell from grace. To be more specific, I fell in love with a woman, and not just any woman. The woman was Martina Navratilova, one of the world's most famous tennis players. Because of her fame and notoriety there was no "coming out" for this newfound lesbian. I was "out" whether I wanted to be or not. The interesting thing is that I never thought of myself as "in" anything. I have, however, come to understand why many gays and lesbians feel they have been or even *must be* in a closet. Society can be cruel and judgmental when it does not understand something. Misunderstandings can be translated into fear. Fear of the unknown can stifle us to the point of distortion, and so it is between the heterosexual and homosexual communities. I speak of distortion because I know from living both a long, healthy heterosexual life and a long and healthy and happy homosexual life that the loving and the family values and the feeling of commitment are the same for both.

Homophobics find it difficult to empathize because they cannot or will not look at homosexuals for the individuals that they are—people living life as their heart dictates. One should never deny one's own heart. I must say that I have never denied my own heart even when I thought it wiser. My choices have been dramatic, my path often difficult, but I have always come out on the other side a stronger and more peaceful person.

What brought this "typical Southern woman" fifty years later to a place where she could reflect upon a unique and unusual life? Perhaps the answer to that question is simply that it is my path. I realize that one can always refuse the path; one can resist change or one can change and grow. I chose to change. Hopefully, I have grown.

Changing does not come easy for Southern girls. A special pattern is handed down from mother to daughter, and the making of that design varies ever so slightly. The rules remain constant. Foremost on the list is goodness. The Southern woman must sacrifice all else to always be thought of as "good." She must display restraint at all times. Anger is not allowed. She must always be charming, unselfishly giving, eternally positive, impeccably polished and clean, never tiring, and always, *always* the perfect ornament for the man in her life. Should she fall short in any of these categories, she is not allowed to let anyone know of it, but rather must march forward with the certainty that she can cook, clean, dance, sing, sew, raise perfect children, and support her perfect man without doubt or fear.

I heard a joke about why Southern women don't like group sex: "Because they'd have to write too many thank-you notes!"

The paradox taught to Southern girls (and certainly the one thing that most perplexed me as I was growing up) is that we are told by our mothers that we can *do* anything. And yet in that very same breath we are told that we also need a "good man to take care of us." That's where I got lost. As many times as I put that in my brain, I could never get it. It just didn't compute. I would say to myself that if I could do anything I wanted, which meant to me that I could take care of myself, then why did I have to have a man (or anyone else for that matter) take care of me? It was a puzzlement.

Being creative as a child, I tried to find ways in which I could please everyone (the second most important lesson for a Southern woman) and still be true to my innermost feelings. This was difficult. For instance, I loved to go barefoot, but good, well-bred girls didn't do that. So I would strike a bargain. Good women always find bargains, so that was allowed and considered appropriate. Therefore, my bargain was to not go barefoot during the school year, but as soon as school was out for the summer, I could play shoeless as long as by evening I would wash my feet and put on my shoes. It was a compromise, but that is one of the things that Southern women do best.

Protocol was always a dress for little girls, so again I had to be creative. If we had to wear dresses to school every day and to church on Sundays, then surely we should have afternoons after school, as well as Saturdays, to wear jeans or shorts, for otherwise the little boys could see our panties when we jumped out of trees while playing Tarzan and Jane. (We always added Jane in there to make the game appropriate for girls, but I will tell you that it was much more fun being Tarzan because he got to swing from vine to vine by himself without any help.)

Yet even with these so-called bargains of mine, I was still often reminded by the generations of women in my family that little girls were to wear dresses and play with dolls. My saving grace was that most all the kids in my neighborhood (many of them cousins) were boys—and they weren't about to play with dolls!

Now, I'm not knocking Southern women. There is a refinement about them that I adore and an innocence that is almost heavenly. I still pride myself in being one of them. I think the values taught are basically healthy ones. If only the part about being a man's ornament and something he can show off at a party, or the part about needing someone else to take care of us, could be deleted, then I think the pattern could be a pretty damn good one. (Oops, strong language is not allowed either, but I promise I only learned to use words like that after I married.)

# CHOICES

# 1

## Growing Up in Texas

I remember it was in fifth grade that I realized I was different. That is not to say that I knew I was a lesbian—I didn't even have that word in my vocabulary. Nor had I ever had sexual feelings about other girls. It was instead a "singling out," so to speak, by my schoolteacher, Mrs. Forest. One day in front of the entire class, she stopped the lesson, having seen some notes being passed among the students. Note passing was her pet peeve, and so it was that this day she would make an issue of the notes and point a chastising finger at Judy Hill, to whom the notes were being directed. These notes were little messages from boys in the class professing their "like" for me above all the other girls. Mrs. Forest would read those notes to the class in some anger and with much disgust, declaring in front of my peers that there were enough girls in the class for every boy, and why then did they *all* have to want *me* for their girlfriend? I was so totally embarrassed and humiliated in front of my friends for being singled out (especially for something so totally out of my control) that I buried my head in my arms on top of my desk and could not bear to look up at anyone.

From that day forward I was different. The other girls in my class became jealous of me. We were much too young to understand such matters. Before that day, jealousy was not something of which I had been aware. I had been innocent and happy—a kid, just a kid who loved to play and enjoy a simple life as only a child knows it.

That happy child was a product of generations of Texans. My grandparents on my mother's side arrived as small children in Fort Worth when it was still a fort. My granddad, Big Pop, told me stories of men wearing six-shooters on their hips, and my grandmother, Big Mama, told me tales of the American Indians who inhabited the surrounding territory. Big Pop was a cowboy. He was short, but his heart made him seem ten feet tall to me. He was a wiry fella with bow legs, weathered skin, a quick smile, and a twinkle in his eye. He was firm but fair (and that was my assessment of him when I was just a young child). He was never judgmental but had a strong sense of right and wrong and a demanding work ethic. He worked and lived off the land. He raised his twelve children that way. He plowed the fields on foot behind two mules. I remember just standing by the fence post and watching him. He was the only person in my early life who never demanded that I be conventional. He taught me a love of the land and of horses. He taught me respect for both. He never drove a car; he always rode a horse. He died when he was eighty-nine and I was nineteen. The vision of that tough little cowboy still lives in my heart, but the gentleness in his soul touches me even today.

He and Big Mama lived just outside of Fort Worth proper. When I was a young girl, I remember going to their house every weekend I had free, just to be around him and to ride a horse—although most of the time it was a mule. My cousin Sharron, who was just a year older, had the same affinity for the country and the horses that I did. When we were about nine or ten, we saved our first dollars and pooled our resources to buy an old mule we named Round as a Log—and that he was! We paid twenty-five dollars for him. We would ride that mule almost every weekend, bareback of course. We would sing, "The old gray mare she ain't what she used to be," and laugh as he jangled us around and about with his very hard trot! We would actually get so tickled with the pure joy of it all that we would begin to slide one way and then the other, all the while trying desperately to hold on. Falling was a long way down for two happy little cowgirls. I think it was at those times that I felt the most free—free to simply be who I was, with no expectations. It is still that way for me today. When I saddle up and get on my horse, I am free. I could be twelve. I could be eighteen. I could be fifty. I feel no sense of age or time.

My mother's mother, Big Mama as we all called her, was not a horsewoman but a woman of the land. She planted and tilled her garden and grew the food the family ate. Having twelve children, she must have been pregnant most of her life. My mother, the next to the youngest of the dozen, was born when Big Mama was forty-five. She lived to the age of eighty-one—died peacefully in her sleep one night. She was a tough little lady. I say little because, unlike the implication of her name, Big Mama was only about five feet tall. I never heard her say a bad word or raise her voice. One had a silent respect for her and always felt that she had everything under control. Wearing a long cotton dress with a cotton bonnet that tied in a bow just under her chin, she would go out into the hot Texas sun and bring in fresh vegetables to be cooked for the noon meal. In her face, the wrinkles and lines told a story of a life of hard work and simple pleasures. Her blue eyes sparkled when she laughed, and her gold tooth, in the upper front, added to the creation of a smile that still lingers in my heart. This tiny, gentle woman was also strong and fearless. She could go out to the chicken coop, grab a chicken, ring its neck, and pluck its feathers before you could say "Scat!" And before you knew it, everyone was sitting down to a meal of down-home cookin' the likes of which you've rarely seen. Even the butter was freshly churned.

In her early seventies Big Mama had a massive stroke. She was not expected to live. But I guess she just wasn't ready to go, because she overcame the life-threatening part and lived the next eight years paralyzed on her right side. She did learn to walk again but never regained the use of her right arm and taught herself to do everything with just her left arm. Remarkable she was.

Big Mama and Big Pop were a remarkable couple. They were a part of this Southern woman's heritage, that part to which at age fifty, I have come full circle—back to my roots, to my soul, to the land and my horses and a more simple sort of life in an often complicated way. This in itself is a contradiction for which I have to find some balance.

Balance, however, for my grandparents was not a therapeutic term; it was an art—the art of balancing the chores, the food, the living space, and the activities of twelve children and staying sane. There were seven girls and five boys. Two of my uncles, Little Joe and Boyce, died before I was born. As a kid, Little Joe was kicked in the head by a horse and died of that injury a few days later. I suspect that is the reason Big Mama never liked horses and also the reason that Big Pop taught me to always have respect for them. Boyce was the youngest of the twelve. He died of stomach cancer at age twenty-one. He was the closest in age of all the kids to my mother, and I think, deep in her heart, she feels the loss even today. He was both her brother and her best friend.

So my mother was the youngest as far as I ever knew. She was named Frances. Mother was essentially raised by her older sisters and brothers. Some of her sisters and brothers were already married when she was born. I think Big Mama must have been tired of raising babies! Of the seven sisters, only one moved away from Texas. The others all stayed, married, and made lots of cousins for me to play with. I had eighteen first cousins just on my mother's side of the family, and *all* of them lived in Forth Worth or close by.

The sisters' names were Lucille, Thelma, Fern, Maxine (or Mickey), Mavis, Golda, and Frances. All were names from a generation of women who watched the world and women's rights change right before their eyes. The brothers were Tot, a cowboy who looked just like Big Pop, Glenn, a Baptist minister, John, Little Joe, and Boyce.

To this day five of the twelve are still living, including my mother, and they all get together at alternating houses to play cards every Wednesday night, beginning with dinner and ending sometime around 2 A.M. It's a card game they call with endearment "crap on your neighbor." And if you really want to laugh until you cry, you should join in on one of those card nights. The stories recounted would make books like *Fried Green Tomatoes* seem tame. Even the grandchildren love to sit in for a hand or two on those evenings just to hear the tales of days gone by and of a generation and a special heritage that is fading.

There is a story about two of the brothers, Tot and Glenn. As memory has it, Tot as a young man became a little envious of his brother Glenn, the preacher, who had just bought a car. Now Tot really wanted a car, so he asked Big Mama how Glenn could afford one. She told him he had bought it with the salary he had made from preaching. So Tot immediately responded by telling Big Mama that he would be a preacher, too. She said that one had to be "called" by the Lord to be a minister. So Tot simply and quickly replied, "I believe I have just been called."

Another story is a wonderful example of how women are capable of finding ways to make things work, no matter what. Fern told me that Big Mama's two daughters Lucille and Thelma were born just eleven months apart, and Big Mama found herself with not enough milk to breast-feed both babies. Her sister-in-law, Aunt Minnie, had just had a baby and, for whatever reason, had an abundance of milk. The two decided it would be perfectly all right for Aunt Minnie to breast-feed Lucille as well as her own baby. This solution worked perfectly and created a special bond between the two women.

Perhaps the most tender of all the tales told to me of Big Pop and big Mama was the story of Little Joe's death. After being kicked in the head by the horse, he was in the hospital for several days before he died. He was only about six years old. They knew from talks with the doctors that Little Joe would not live. They were a proud family and wanted an appropriate burial for Little Joe. He had had no shoes. Little Joe had wanted a pair of tennis shoes, but they were not affordable. Big Pop and Big Mama did not want him to be buried without any shoes. So Big Pop got on his horse and rode into town. No one knows what he had to sell to get the money, but Little Joe was buried in a pair of brand-new tennis shoes. That was love. That was sacrifice. I wept when I heard that story.

On the other side of the family, my father's parents were also two remarkable people—more citified but still people of integrity and strong wills, who lived life with a pureness and an honesty rarely witnessed today. A plate of hard work was always on the menu. That generation of people just seemed to know that hard work was a part of life. Complaining about it was pointless. One just did whatever one had to do to make things work—a philosophy and a work ethic upon which I was teethed.

My father's dad was a postman most of his life, carrying the mail on foot from house to house. In his twenties and thirties he was also a circuit preacher, driving his horse and buggy from one church to another in the more rural areas that surrounded Fort Worth. He volunteered his spare time to the brotherhood of the Boy Scouts and was a scoutmaster for forty-five years.

But what I remember most about him were his hands. He had strong, supple, creative hands. He could make seemingly anything out of scraps of leather. With an assortment of tiny tools he would emboss designs on the belts and wallets that he made. He was also an expert fisherman. I heard many tales about the ones that got away. But, you know, I really did believe him. That was just the kind of man he was.

He had a collection of *National Geographic* magazines that stood in rows stacked higher than my head, and he had read every word in them and journeyed into every photograph. It was his fantasy, I think, his way of doing the traveling that he never got to do. If ever I needed materials for a report at school, he knew precisely where to find the article. I always had the best reports thanks to him.

He stood about six feet tall, with grayish hair usually combed neatly to the side and in his later years trimmed short in a kind of flattop. He wore thick glasses because as he grew older, he developed cataracts. They almost blinded him until he finally had them surgically removed. But I remember that he could still thread fishhooks as though his fingers were his eyes. I wish I had spent more time fishing with him, but that was a "boy thing" back home and so I was seldom invited along.

My grandmother was fondly referred to simply as Grannie. She was the purest, sweetest, most giving person God ever put on this earth. She was four feet eleven inches tall at most, yet had a presence that filled an entire room. She never stopped working (a trait my mother displays to this day). If she ever sat down, she immediately picked up her soft knitting bag, filled with strands of yarn in all colors and textures and an assortment of needles to rival a tailor's. As she sat in her favorite chair, she would weave her magic like a spider spinning its web. She would crochet delicate doilies or baby shoes or tablecloths or lovely collars for dresses yet to be sewn.

I have seen picture of her as a young lady, and she was quite stunning. She and my dad actually looked a lot alike when they were young. I would describe them both as handsome. But Grannie as I knew her had soft white hair that she wore short and all brushed back from her face in what we used to call finger waves. She always wore dresses, with hemlines just below midcalf. She wore stockings, carefully rolled down to just below her knees, and tiny black leather shoes that laced up and had thick, squatty heels. She carried a purse that eternally contained a pack of Dentyne gum. She would give each of us (the grand-children) a piece every Sunday during the sermon at church in exchange for a promise not to talk during the service. Our fam-ily—grandparents, parents, aunts, uncles, cousins, brothers, and sisters—all sat together in the same two pews every Sunday. Going to church on Sunday and on Wednesday nights was a way of life for all of us. It was my grandmother's only activity outside the home. She was a fixture there. We were all Methodist, although my mother had been brought up in the Baptist Church.

Grannie had five children. One of the daughters died at eighteen months of whooping cough. Two of them, Sonny and Sister, as they were called, were twins. There was another daughter, Inez, and my dad, Sargent (my grandmother's maiden name), was the youngest. They were all born at home.

When I was growing up, every Sunday after church we would all go to Grannie's for Sunday lunch. It was always a feast to behold. My grandmother was a wonderful cook—that is, if you enjoy country cooking. She could fry up a skillet of okra that I can taste even today if I just close my eyes.

On Saturday nights during the long, hot summers in Texas, the family—aunts, uncles, and cousins included—would all sit out in the backyard at Grannie's, and the kids would take turns sitting on the ice cream freezer as one of the adults turned the handle round and round until the sweet mixture became soft and creamy. Each of us kids would sit until his buns got so cold that he couldn't stand it any longer, then would jump up so the next kid could take over. All the while the other children would be running around catching lightning bugs, as we called them, and putting them in clear-glass bell jars with lids that we had punched holes in with an ice pick. Their flickering, golden lights contrasted against the darkness of the navy blue sky, cre-ating a make-believe world of peaceful, happy, carefree faces of kids who did not know such words as *crime* or *rape* or *drugs*. These were nights of innocent bliss. We all grew up.

It is as though I am meant to remember vividly the innocence of childhood to keep myself grounded, as the paths I
have taken have not been easy, and the life not simple. I have
been uprooted so many times, and yet I yearn for the earthy,
uncomplicated roots of my heritage. Perhaps that is why just
reflecting on the little red leather moccasins like the Indians
wore, a present from my parents on my second birthday, gives
me such joy. I've often wondered why I remember that gift
more than other, more expensive gifts of birthdays past and also
why I am able to recall strong feelings from such a young age.
It is as if it is a piece of me—a very important piece.

As a child the most simple things always gave me the most
pleasure. Playing games with the other kids in the neighborhood, such as kick the can and hide-and-seek and murder in
the dark—games that required nothing but a bunch of kids and
their imaginations.

I was aware by the age of five that life on the outside was
more complicated. By that I mean that I began to realize that
the rules for girls and boys were different. I didn't like it. Even
though I could physically and mentally keep up with every boy
on the block, both the spoken and unspoken message to me
from the adults in my life (except for Big Pop) was that I was
not supposed to show that I could do things and be as smart or
as fast as the boys. If I was, and I was, I certainly had to pull
back—the rationale being that, if I was better or smarter than
the boys were, then they would not like me as a girlfriend.
Even at age five the message was that my job was to be pretty
and proper and to always, always let the boy win. I had a really
hard time with this philosophy. It just didn't seem fair. But all
the women who influenced my life were very definite about
this rule, and even my father and brother agreed when I questioned its validity that indeed boys did not like (as their girlfriends) girls who could do things better or as well as they
could do them. So I held back—even at age five. Internally I
was angry, but good little girls were not ever to show anger.

Therefore the rage and questioning just settled inside me. One day—many years later—I would face those contradictions and double standards head-on.

I was always being groomed to be the good girl, the good student, the good wife and the good mother. Many pretty little girls in Texas are groomed from an early age to be Miss America. The seed is planted and the garden cultivated—which includes some type of voice or dance lessons every year—until she reaches the appropriate age to enter the contest. I was no exception. I took "Voice and Expression." Even though I could not sing, I was asked to sing at all family gatherings—an awful experience. I did it because it was what I was supposed to do. I hated it, but I never said no. I also had to sing at recitals and talent shows, a mortifying experience. But supposedly practice made perfect, and one day I might be Miss America. I never was, but I did become the National Maid of Cotton in 1965. I traveled around the world for a year promoting the cotton industry by doing fashion shows and television and radio interviews and making speeches wherever I went. It changed my life. That's a story all its own. Anyway, for everyone—family, friends, and community—that honor was good enough, so I never had to try out for Miss America. I was, however, asked to judge the Miss Texas Pageant the year that Phyllis George won. She went on to win the Miss America title. I was twenty years old and the *only* woman on the panel of "good ole boy" judges.

Speaking of good ole boys, I remember being aware at an early age that boys had the power. They were in control. Looking back, I realize that at age four or five I devised a way to have the power when playing with my girlfriends. Little girls were supposed to play with dolls, not marbles and stick horses, which I got to do anyway thanks to the fact that most of the kids in my neighborhood were boys. God must have done me that favor. My mother and grandmother insisted that I ask for a doll from Santa Claus at Christmas. This was the only appropriate request that little girls could make. I asked for a *boy* doll. In my life I had only two dolls—both boys. That way when I *had* to play dolls with the other girls, I had the power. My doll could be the doctor, the lawyer, or the football player. Theirs had to be the nurse, the secretary, or the cheerleader. I could tell them all what to do. Thank you, Gloria Steinem, for helping to change that concept.

Growing up, I played a lot with the boys, at least as much as I was allowed. I was, however, aware that my parents wished I would spend more time with other little girls. Frankly I found them boring and somewhat lazy. I wanted to be outside playing and jumping and running. I often joined my brother and his pals for cowboys and Indians, Tarzan and Jane, and army.

My brother is two years older than I. I always thought he was a pretty cool guy to let me play with him and the fellas, because most of the time I was the only girl allowed. That made me feel really special—as if I could almost do or be anything I wanted. But I was careful never to get too cocky or I would instantly be reminded that I was just a girl and should consider myself lucky to be included in their games. I was walking a tightrope, and I was always careful to maintain my balance.

My brother was a good kid. Most of the time I liked him. We would have the usual brother-and-sister spats. At those times I learned to fear his anger. He was stronger, and he frightened me when he would lose his temper. We were not always the perfect, good kids. We did try hard, though, never to let anyone outside the immediate family know that we were ever bad.

There was one incident, however, when my brother and I were about fourteen and twelve respectively, that I remember vividly. I had deliberately damaged one of the airplanes, which he had carefully assembled out of balsa wood, that hung from the ceiling of his room. That was considered bad. In a rage, he came bounding into my room threatening to kill me. Picking up the BB gun on the floor beside me, I said, "If you come any closer to me, I'll shoot you in the leg." He didn't believe me, of course, until he felt the undeniable sting of the BB that pierced and lodged in his skin just above the knee. Like a wild, wounded animal, he charged me with a vengeance. Scared to death, I dodged his death-defying leap and ran screaming for my mother's protection. This was about as deliberately bad as I ever remember being. I felt guilty about that for years and wondered from where my uncontrolled anger had come.

We had, and still have, this tacit code of silence in my family. If you do anything—or anything happens to you—that is less than admirable, you simply do not discuss it. The important thing is always to appear happy, good, and as picture-perfect as possible. Therefore, anything less than "good," which would of course be interpreted as "bad," would disappear. Breaking this code of silence at age thirty-eight, I did something very public that was considered inappropriate. I changed my life to live openly with a woman. That's another chapter.

So powerful is this code in my life and within my family that to this very day no soul other than my parents has ever known of one incident in my early childhood. At age six, I was sexually molested by a sixteen-year-old boy. He lived in my neighborhood only a few houses down from mine and was giving me a ride on his bicycle. He had a boy's bike with a bar between the seat and the handlebars, and you could sit on it sort of sidesaddle fashion. As he was giving me a ride, I felt his fingers move inside my panties and he began to fondle me. I was frozen. I was scared to death. In a tingling kind of way it felt good, and in another way it was the most horrifying feeling in my life. I knew it was a bad thing. I knew he should not be touching me down there. It was wrong. I could not speak. I could not scream. I just wanted to get off that bike and run as fast as I could to my house and never come out again. I think I must have told him that I had to go home and jumped off the bicycle. I ran and never looked back.

As a matter of fact I never looked at that boy again in my life. How I avoided that, I am not clear. I just remember that

I never walked near his house again. After about a year he moved away. I cannot even tell you his name or recall what he looked like, and I have an excellent memory. The experience was powerful, demeaning, embarrassing, and humiliating. Nobody knew of this except my parents until now.

Why now? Because I think it is time that someone in my family breaks that code of silence. The rationale behind the code of silence is that if you don't talk about it, then one day you won't remember that it even happened. I think it's time for me to finally say, I'm not bad because that happened to me, and my family should not be ashamed because of it. What really should have happened is that someone should have become mad, made known what the boy had done, and *he* should have been punished and humiliated for it, not me, not my family.

I still have a lot invested in being well perceived, but I do think I've come a long way in detaching myself from that burdensome way of life—thinking that anything less than perfection is failure. My shoulders are just not broad enough to carry that load. Realizing this, I still found it difficult to reveal my sexual abuse. This is mainly due to what I will call my "aha theory." You know, "Aha, so *that's* why she's a lesbian!" But that theory won't hold water because millions of women have been sexually abused, with more coming forward every day, and the majority of them are heterosexuals. I am a lesbian because it's what I feel in my heart. I like, love, and enjoy being in the company of and sharing my life and intimacies with a woman. It is fulfilling. It is for me. It is not for everyone, nor is heterosexuality for everyone.

Actually, for as long as I was a heterosexual, I think I was a pretty good one. Sure I had my "terrible Judy" moments that I am at last willing to look at and say, "Yep, I did that, made that mistake." But I'm not a bad person or a failure because of it, nor, God forbid, do I mind that anyone else should know of it. I liked boys. As I grew up, I fell in love with some men. I probably dated more than the average girl because to date a lot meant that you were popular. Being popular was extremely important to the image that I was taught to pursue. It also meant that other girls would be jealous. But it was better to have girls jealous of you than not to be popular with the guys. One day you would fall in love and marry and you would not have a girl in your life in that way—so ultimately what the boys thought of you was more important. Little did I know then that there would be women in my life in a romantic capacity. If I had known, I'd have paid more attention to them when I was growing up!

Actually I have always had strong feelings for my girl-friends. I still do. These, however, are not romantic feelings. Lesbians are *not* romantically involved with every woman they love and cherish. We have girlfriends just like heterosexual women. That probably shatters another myth. The bond that I have formed with women friends throughout my life has been extremely important to me. And just in case any of my sorority sisters ever reads this book, I will tell you now to put your mind at ease. I was not looking at you with some sexual desire. You were my friends, just friends, and I did not ever fantasize about you as lovers.

My thoughts as a teenager were of being a cheerleader, homecoming queen, the yearbook beauty, "Miss This, Miss That." Good grades were also important, but that was taken for granted. It was part of the criteria for being a good girl. If you didn't make the honor roll, you certainly didn't broadcast it.

I remember my first kiss. I was in the third grade. My boyfriend (*one* of them ... but the most special one), Rocky Martin, decided to do it, so we planned the moment. We were at his house after school one day. He had an old boat in his backyard with a tarp thrown over it. We crawled into the boat and pulled the cover over us and closed our eyes and kissed on the lips. It lasted about half a second. I was so afraid I would miss his mouth because my eyes were shut, but somehow we pulled it off. We were so proud of ourselves. It made us feel all grown-up and surely "in love"—because you only kiss when you are in love with the person. After that I kissed a lot of toads before I found my princess!

On the other hand, Frances Bales, my mom, found herself a prince. His name was Sargent Hill, my dad, and he had found a princess. They have been married for fifty-five years. I will never be able to break that record, but I cannot think of two more worthy people to hold it.

Mother is gentle and strong, giving and creative. She has the attributes of both her parents, and I adore her. Yet, try as I may, I will never be like her. She is of a generation whose rules of right and wrong, of goodness and sin, and of "sticking it out" even to the loss of self are beyond where I am willing to compromise any longer. What worked for her and her generation does not necessarily work for me and mine. I must be true to my own heart, taking from the lessons of my parents the things that work for me and discarding those things that do not.

My mom is lovely to look at, with blue eyes the color of the sea. She has always been a stylish woman, with taste and a sense of design that enable her to always be appropriately dressed and well-groomed. The gold of Big Mama's tooth must have been placed in my mother's heart, for truly hers is made of it. She has an innocence about her that I believe was passed on to my younger sister, Jan. I don't have it, though. I do think I am a bit naïve, as is my mom. At times that gets us into trouble because we are so trusting and accepting. On the other hand, at times I find the trait endearing, especially in my mother.

Like my daddy's mother, my mom does not know how to just sit. Even in stillness she finds something to do, like ironing or mending holes in the jeans of all her grandkids. These are two things—ironing and sewing—I have chosen *not* to learn. I used to wonder why. I think I now know.

My father is her prince, her knight in shining armor. He is, and always was, a most handsome man. He proudly has all of his beautiful white hair. Before he went prematurely gray in his early forties, his hair was jet-black. He has a quick smile and can sit and tell endless stories of adventure, especially of airplanes. We still laugh every time we hear about his flying my mother upside down in an open-cockpit plane when she was pregnant. I can't even imagine what that would feel like. I just know that it displays both courage and trust.

He was a good athlete in school, winning letters in almost every sport. In college he was a speech and drama major, always playing the dashing leading man. Like his father, he is good with his hands. When I was little, he made most of our toys, like scooters and wagons and tree houses.

He and my mom loved to dance, although my dad's parents considered it a sin. It was, I think, the only thing my parents did that was forbidden. They would sneak off to the Casino, a large club on Lake Worth, to dance to the big-band sounds of such greats as Jimmy Dorsey and Glenn Miller. It was a nostalgic era—a time of lovers and dreamers. They still steal the show when they get out on the dance floor. Like me when I ride my horse, they could be twelve. They could be eighteen. They could be fifty. I love that about them. I, too, love to dance with Daddy.

I do love to dance, even now. I love to go dancing with the girls (an option I've only enjoyed in the past couple of years). I love dancing with my sons, Eddie and Bales. And I love to dance with my lover.

I remember the first boy I ever danced "close" with—Chip Raymond. We were in the sixth grade, and my family and I had moved to Nashville, Tennessee. This temporary move proved to be a great experience for all my family because we had not really known a world outside of Texas. Chip was my boyfriend of the moment. We began dancing in a traditional slow-dance fashion, but barely touching each other. Before the night was over we were dancing cheek to cheek. I remember our cheeks stuck together at the end of the dance because we were so hot and sweaty from the fast dances in between. At that time I had no inkling of wanting to dance with a girl in that way.

Girls did dance with girls though. It was the best way to learn new dance steps. After school the boys were always at football or basketball practice, and the girls would congregate at one house or another to watch *American Bandstand*, hosted by Dick Clark. The first dance show on TV, it was live every weekday from Philadelphia. The kids who danced on the show to all the most popular songs became "regulars" so to speak, as they appeared daily, and even became celebrities of sorts, appearing on the covers of *Sixteen* and *Teen* magazines. Many entertainers got their start on that show, such as Paul Anka, Neil Sedaka, Frankie Avalon, Fabian, Annette Funicello, and Connie Francis.

My girlfriends and I were faithful viewers, watching intently so that we could pick up on every new dance step. At parties on the weekends, we would teach the steps to the guys. Usually the girls were better partners. The boys seemed to have things on their minds other than executing the proper dance technique.

One summer, two of the most popular girls on *American Bandstand*, Arlene Sullivan and Barbara Levick, came to visit some friends in Arlington, Texas (a town close to Fort Worth). A girlfriend in our circle was introduced to Arlene and Barbara. She, in turn, invited them over to a slumber party at my house. Much to our joy and excitement and disbelief, Arlene and Barbara showed up. Wow. That was really big-time. We stayed up all night and we learned all the newest dance steps firsthand. It was better than being on television. And they were at *my* house. We all had so much fun that we talked them into staying several more days before returning to Philadelphia. They stayed with my family. After they left, we became pen pals with them and watched *Bandstand* with more exuberance than ever.

Later that same summer my family and I took a vacation to New York. I talked them into going back through Philadelphia so that I could visit Arlene and Barbara. Not only did I get to do that, but I got to be on *American Bandstand!* I was even interviewed by Dick Clark as Arlene and Barbara sat beside me telling stories of how we all met in Texas and what fun we had had. The best part of all was that Kenny Rossi, Arlene's steady boyfriend and dance partner, asked me to dance! I danced with Kenny on TV with all my friends back home watching with both joy and envy. What a dream! But that's not the end of the story. Some thirty years later, after I had appeared on the Phil Donahue show during my book tour with my first book, *Love Match, Nelson vs. Navratilova*, written with Sandra Faulkner, my editor, Allan Wilson at Carol Publishing Group, received a phone call from a woman named Arlene Sullivan. She asked only that he refer the call to me and asked that if I remembered her, would I return the call. Did I remember her! I was thrilled and amazed. I called her. She said that when they referred to me as Judy Hill and gave my family's names from the book, she knew instantly that I was the same Judy Hill whom she had visited so many years ago back in Texas. We laughed and giggled as if we were sixteen again. She never married Kenny. They remain friends to this day. She discovered that she preferred the company of women. Ah, life's little ironies.

My first real love happened in the eighth grade. Kurt Meer was in the seventh grade, but because he was old for his grade and I was young for mine (I started in the first grade when I was only five), we were only one month apart in age. We dated and went steady off and on until I was a freshman in college. All of my first real sexual experiences were with Kurt. That is not to say that we made love or, as we said back then, "went all the way." We did not. There again was another rule of my Southern upbringing: simply put, "good girls didn't and bad girls did." It was not a fine line. It was a huge boundary. I never crossed that boundary until I met my husband. He was the first man I ever made love to—again the perfect Southern girl who "saved" herself for her husband. Today, I find the reasons artificial, but the principle a good one. There is, however, something to be said for experience, or maybe satisfying love-making is a combination of experience and trust and freedom of expression.

My sense of right and wrong, taught to me by my parents, was what kept me on the path of the "straight and narrow" (pun intended!). It was a righteous path. The only problem I had with it was that somehow it was not so rigid for the boys. What was known as the double standard in my generation was forever prevalent. I was furious about it. I didn't understand why girls who veered from the path of righteousness were "sluts" and the boys who dabbled in premarital sex were just "good ole boys" experimenting. Supposedly they were doing it for the good of the girls because it would make them better lovers for their wives. I don't think so. But if that were true, what then were the guys getting with their sweet virgins? Mothers?

Much to my parents' credit (I think), they at least were con-sistent with the rules. What was good for the gander was good for the goose. Therefore, my brother was expected to live by the same sexual code that I was taught. He was a good boy. He was also always quick to tell me when I was dating a guy who might possibly want more than I could give him sexually.

So stringent were the rules of right and wrong and of good and bad that I was always clear on which side of the line I was standing. There was no chance for ambivalence. Because of my strong sense of honor and my commitment to religious values instilled in me from birth, I was sometimes referred to as Jesus Judy. When I was a senior in high school, some kids stuck a cross into the ground in my front yard that had those words written on it. On one hand I loved being thought of as good, for that was my duty in life, yet on the other hand I was be-ginning to be old enough to feel the rigidity that it implied. I sloughed it off by saying it was nice to be considered in such good company. On the inside I was beginning to feel the pres-sure imposed by "the perfect-image syndrome"—especially when I knew that I wasn't perfect and was never allowed to admit it.

In gallant pursuit of my designated goodness, I, at age sixteen, decided that I wanted to be a missionary when I grew up. This was entirely acceptable to my family, although I think they did think it was a bit far-fetched for this Southern girl, who would always need a good man to take care of her. In retrospect I think it was my subconscious devising a brilliant way for both travel and self-sufficiency to be acceptable for a woman. Although not the norm, it was a creative calling that would fulfill my needs to be on my own and take care of myself. Those two needs were never to be met until now. I was not fully aware that those *were* my needs until I was stripped bare both emotionally and monetarily. I finally got the message. I am now on a journey to prove to myself that I can take care of myself—a message, remember, that good Southern girls are never given.

As a young college girl, I was *not* in pursuit of the lessons of life. I concentrated only on the lessons in my books. I was, as usual, a good student without too much effort. College was supposed to be the Southern girl's last chance to have fun and find her husband while Daddy still paid the bills. That was the message a lot of us received, although of course some students in college with me had higher expectations from education. I did not neglect the other important message about college, which was that I was also there to receive my "security diploma." That meant at the end of four years I was to hold in my hands a certificate that would enable me to teach school should anything, God forbid, ever happen to my husband, like a heart attack or an automobile accident. Divorce was not an openly discussed option. Girls who are good wives and mothers and lovers never get divorced. That is a given. Good begets good.

While Jane Fonda was protesting the war in Vietnam, and Gloria Steinem and Rita Mae Brown were out marching for my rights, I was at Texas Christian University being the Howdy

Week Queen and pledging the Tri Delta sorority. Thank goodness that I've gotten a second chance as I enter my second adulthood to stand up for more than just an applauding audience. In an odd way, my public life with Martina created some recognition (some negative, some positive) that now enables me to discuss my issues on a broader scale. I thank Martina for that.

The fact is, however, that I was a very public person long before I ever met Martina. I was just not willing to be political for fear that my views might not be acceptable to everyone and might hurt me and my family. Whatever I did to change things was to be done silently so as never to cause conflict—never "rock the boat."

Even when I was selected as the 1965 National Maid of Cotton, the message to me from the Cotton Council was to always be personally and politically correct. I was not to make statements that would raise eyebrows. I do wonder from time to time what that organization must think of me now—a lesbian Maid of Cotton! Strange when I think of it, because just that mere fact does not change the way I look, or talk, or act, or dress. I am still just plain Judy.

I became the twenty-seventh National Maid of Cotton when I was a sophomore in college. I was only nineteen. I was the youngest Maid of Cotton ever selected. Overnight I became a public figure. I would spend the next nine months on a world tour in the company of kings and queens, movie stars, politicians, and even the president of the United States. I would be recognized and given "keys" to the places I visited by governors and mayors.

I returned to college at TCU a different person. I was a woman of the world, older and wiser. To make up for lost time at school, I had to take a heavy load of classes to catch up with my classmates. Even carrying extra hours, the maximum permitted each semester, I would graduate in summer school just after my class had graduated in the spring. But, by damn, I had done it in four years! Some things in me had not changed. Ridding oneself of the arbitrary rules one is taught from birth, or changing the pattern even the slightest, is most difficult for a good Southern girl.

The summer after my year as the Maid of Cotton, I desperately wanted to get back to some kind of "normal" life, as I called it. I was tired of the interviews and the magazine covers (at least in Texas) and the constant requests for public appearances back home. I was different, but I wanted to be just plain Judy again.

I took a job for part of that summer as a camp counselor at a girl's camp called Waldemar, located in the hill country outside of Austin, Texas. It proved to be a good change of pace. I got to be outdoors and was surrounded by young campers who didn't really know who I was until they would write home about me and their parents would recognize the name. But it wasn't a big deal to the kids. I just taught them how to play golf. Later, after they found out that I was a sort of celebrity, they would ask me questions about my experiences and travels. I would tell them stories and they would dream their own dreams. I think they were always happy to see that I was a regular girl.

I think they were more interested at times in my boyfriend, who would drive down on the weekends to visit me. He was a young dentist (as I was now dating "older men") from Fort Worth. He was tanned and handsome, with blond hair and the bluest eyes, and a blue Corvette convertible to match. I actually thought a lot about marrying him. The timing was not right. It was just too soon. I had college to finish. That was the plan.

Sometimes it is only in retrospect that you fully realize the significance of events in your life. Such was my experience at Camp Waldemar. Among those young campers was a girl named Susan Spears. She was five years younger, the same age as my sister. I became almost as close to Susan and her family as I was to mine. We have now been friends for almost thirty years. Susan is the godmother of my two sons, and she now has four beautiful children of her own. My son Eddie was the ringbearer at her wedding. They live in Houston, and although I am unable to see Susan and Ted, her husband, and the children as much as I would like, the bond of friendship we formed that summer so long ago has grown as we have.

After my summer at Waldemar I returned to TCU. The remaining two years of college went by quickly. I dated a lot of guys, still looking for Mr. Right. I enjoyed the attention of my suitors, but did not think I had found my Prince Charming. My mother tells me she still has a letter that Pat Boone sent to me after he and I cohosted the Maid of Cotton selection in Memphis the following year. In the letter he reveals his less than proper (he was married) romantic intentions. I didn't know until recently that the letter still existed.

Troy Donahue, an actor and teenage heartthrob of my generation, was another of my fancy flings—a one-nighter. We met while staying at the same hotel in Flagstaff, Arizona. He was on location making a film, and I was on my way back from a trip to California with my mother, aunts, and cousin. When Mother recalls the date, I laugh until I cry. She, of course, remembers many more details about the evening than I, but I remember the kisses in his car after we came back to the hotel after dinner. He was dating Suzanne Pleshette at the time, but they were having a lovers' quarrel or so he said. I think he married Suzanne a year later for a brief time.

The fact is I like dating. I like the attention. I wish that lesbians did more dating before settling down into a relationship. However, I think that society's prejudices make that a bit difficult because women who are obviously gay are stared at and looked upon as being odd or abnormal. Therefore, dating and holding hands and looking lovingly at each other in public for lesbians is not usually an easy prospect.

When I look back on my heterosexual privileges, I realize there are other things I miss because being in love with a woman is still not entirely acceptable to the public. I miss holding hands freely. I miss dancing close, cheeks touching and heart pounding. I miss kisses of pure joy. I miss long, deep looks into the eyes of the one I love. I do all of these things in public sometimes, but I am always careful not to make someone who is homophobic uncomfortable. Maybe one day I won't have to think about that at all. I wish.

During those last couple of years at TCU, I became very involved in the activities of my sorority, Delta Delta Delta. Even Rita Mae Brown pledged that one! My senior year I became the pledge trainer, the person responsible for teaching all the new pledges the history of our prestigious sorority and its purpose. I was directly responsible for the attitudes, grades, happiness, and collegiate values of some twenty or more young girls—or so it seemed. I took my responsibilities seriously, as I always did. Oddly enough, it was through this experience that I met my husband-to-be, Eddie Nelson, as he was called in college. He didn't become known as Ed until sometime early in medical school when he was first paged at the hospital as Dr. Eddie Nelson. He said the moment he heard that, he knew it was time to be called Ed.

Ed and I met when we were both seniors. We had both gone to TCU all four years but had never met. He was the vice president of the student body and president of his fraternity, the Delts. They were our "brother" fraternity, and for that reason we had scheduled a "pledge party" together. Being the pledge trainer, I organized the party between our girls and their boys. Although the pledges were usually all freshman, the pledge trainers and other officers were traditionally required to attend. One of my girlfriends in my sorority knew Ed and told me about him. She said he was handsome and smart and all the other right things. She thought I would like him. There was one big problem. I had never been on a blind date and had no desire to go on one. I wanted to date based on my own judgment, not someone else's. I said No—gracefully, of course. I went to the party with one of the few Delts I did know.

I usually dated either SAEs or Kappa Sigs. It all seems like such silly stuff now, but at the time it was hugely important—as it was all about popularity and dating the boys in just the "right" fraternity. It was about image. Only many years later would I blow that all to hell.

Ed showed up at the party with one of my prettiest sorority sisters. I was a bit jealous even though I didn't even know him. All night long I "checked him out," as we used to say. Yes, he was handsome. He couldn't dance very well, but I thought that was just because he seemed self-conscious when trying. He had a nice build, which meant "body" in my day, and he generally was well put together. I kept an eye on him and at the end of the evening I remember lingering downstairs in the Tri Delta house to see him bring his date in from the party. In the entry hall, he gave her a little kiss on the lips to say good night. I watched and found myself being just a little jealous, again.

I called my sorority sister the next morning—the one that had tried to get me to go out with Ed—and told her that now that I had seen him, I *would* like to go out with him sometime. She told him. He called that same evening. He asked me to the next Saturday football game. I accepted, then immediately picked up the phone to break the date with the boy with whom I had already promised to see the game. I didn't like breaking dates. Sometimes a girl just had to do it. That would be the last date I would ever break.

It was love. Eddie Nelson was the man of my dreams. It was just as my mom had always told me when I asked her how I would know when to marry. She would always just say, "You'll know." I did.

I stopped dating anyone else. Two weeks later we were "dropped," which was the equivalent of going steady in high school. (I'm not sure that term was any more sophisticated. I wonder where we got those phrases anyway!) After three months we were pinned. That is where the girl wears the boy's fraternity pin. It's a big deal. All the fraternity and sorority brothers and sisters join in a ceremony in which you sing frat songs to each other in honor of the loving couple's pledge. After six months we were engaged to be married. He gave me an engagement ring, which we designed with the help of the jeweler. It had a center diamond with smaller sapphires all around it. It was not the traditional solitary diamond on a thin band. This could have been my family's first hint that I was not always going to be traditional. But I bet they missed it! For that matter, so did I.

On Valentine's Day, appropriately as always, we announced our engagement and he slipped the ring on my finger. We were both twenty-one and all grown up. We married almost a year later on December 16, 1967. We were twenty-two. Ed was a first-year medical student, and I was teaching school. The plan for my life was followed exactly. All was perfect. Young, happy, handsome, and smart—we had the world on a string.

# 2

## The Beautiful and Good: Southern Women

Southern women are born female and bred to be Southern. When I was born, I was almost named Baby Hill, as the story is told. My father, a flying instructor during the war, was in Denver when I was born on September 17, 1945. As soon as he was notified of my birth, he took leave and headed for Fort Worth. He was a couple of days late, and on the very day that he arrived, the hospital administrative office had threatened to put "Baby" Hill on my birth certificate if my mother did not give me a name. She emphatically replied that she would not give me a name until my father arrived. She had to consult him because they had not yet selected any name for a girl. He arrived in the nick of time and together they agreed that they would name me after the prettiest and most popular girl they had known in school: Judy. They told me that they really didn't know the girl well. I do wonder what would have happened had they named me after the smartest girl they had known instead.

I, like most Southern women, had much invested in being perceived as good. I therefore spent most of my life trying to be just that. I remember a little poem that my mother used to recite to me as a child:

*There was a little girl*
*Who had a curl*
*Right in the middle of her forehead.*
*And when she was good,*
*She was very, very good*
*And when she was bad,*
*She was horrid.*

That was the deal—either you were a good girl, or a bad one, and there was no in between.

A good Southern woman is also taught that her beauty is her power. A woman's success depends on her looks and charm, not her brain and resourcefulness. The fallacy of course is that beautiful women are then generally dependent. The power of beauty gets her by until midlife when her beauty begins to fade. Since she has always gotten by on her looks, she, more often than not, was not trained to use her brain and then sadly never learns to become self-sufficient. The Southern man, meanwhile, wants a beautiful woman as an ornament to show off to the other guys—the idea being that he must have something special (money, body, brain) to have attracted this gorgeous woman. She is able to hold him in her grasp as long as she possesses this cachet. When her beauty fades, more often than not, he leaves her for a younger model in order to reestablish his importance. The wilting daisy is left to dry out by some swimming pool all alone. She is reduced to searching for the latest in cosmetics and plastic surgery. Of that, I am as guilty as anyone. It is just now that I have found intelligence useful and much more dependable, providing me with some newfound security and courage.

I have never considered myself beautiful, but because I have this certain way about me—I think it's the way everything's put together—people look. Martina was quoted once as saying that I "turn heads." But I say now, what good is that if you can't use your own head?

I was taught that my looks and charm could open doors. Sadly, they did. I have used both to my advantage most of my life. This has often put me above and before others. It is a facade for which people clamor; it is not real. It creates a conditioned dependency. We get gifts for just existing. Men do things for us merely to have us around them. I often feel Martina did that, too. I didn't think about it at the time, but upon reflection on the dynamics of that relationship, I see the evidence. When she left, she did so for many reasons, but I believe she also wanted a younger model.

Being beautiful is something that one usually has no control over, and if one is taught properly from the "Good Southern Woman" handbook as I call it, it can dominate one's entire life. I think a curse surrounds this particular Southern beauty concept. I found this in my relationship with men: they all wanted something more than just friendship. Friendship was what I most often had to offer; *good* Southern girls are supposed to offer their bodies only to one man. Therefore the curse is that I could never have any male friends. They all eventually wanted more than I was willing to give them. Only now do I have some real male friends, and most of them are gay except for one—a special man and friend in my life, Travis Critzer.

I said earlier that as I was growing up, I realized men had the power. As I got older, I realized that was not entirely true. Southern women are taught to always make the man feel important and that he has control, but the unspoken truth is that if she plays her cards right, she holds the reins. But she must never, never let him know. I am, however, certain that I have not revealed any secret that my daddy, deep down inside, has not known for many years. If he has not known this secret until now, I apologize to you, Mother, for letting the cat out of the bag.

My sister, Jan, almost five years younger than I, is the epitome of the beautiful and good Southern woman. I mean that as a compliment from the bottom of my heart. The difference here is that she really loves being considered that. There is no facade about her. She is the most charming, innocent person; yet on the inside, like my mom, she is tough as nails. It's sort of like the slogan "Don't mess with Texas." Well, don't mess with Jan either. She's got a brain and she doesn't see any reason to let the fellas know it until she just has to—and at that point she already has them eating out of her lovely hands and lost in her wonderful blue eyes. She uses her Southern good looks and charm in a most endearing way. She is satisfied with her life and her looks. She works hard at running the household and maintaining balance. She makes things flow. Don't cross the lady or inside you'll find a tiger. I love that about her. Hats off to my sister.

Hats off to the good Southern women who have found they have a brain, even if they hide it until absolutely necessary.

# 3

## The Good Ole Boys: Southern Men

Down home, the "nineteenth hole" refers to a bar and dining area at the country club where only the guys are admitted. No women allowed. Never have been. Never will be, I suspect. That's where the good ole boys meet after a round of golf to have a beer or just to play gin rummy or to get away from their wives, or possibly all three.

The women golfers, on the other hand, were relegated to the basic mixed-grill room where both sexes could congregate for a bite to eat: chicken-salad sandwiches or fruit salad and an iced tea for the ladies and burgers and beer for the guys.

If the issue of the nineteenth hole's being exclusively for the men was not enough to get me charged up, then the fact that no blacks or Jews were allowed membership in my country club was. My good-girl upbringing must have prohibited me from being very political when I was a member. Today I would choose not to be a member because of the club's discriminatory practices. In actuality, I found out in a "bassackwards" sort of way after my divorce that I could no longer be a member of that club anyway. In my divorce settlement, I was to receive the club membership, which had some monetary value. However, to my shock and surprise I found that I could not receive the membership because a single woman was not allowed to be a member! Only through her husband could she gain admittance. Wow. I hope that policy has been changed as well. I've never, however, felt the need to rejoin in order to find out. That was and is a past life.

Speaking of past lives, I love those guys back home. They have a certain charm and graciousness about them that is distinctly Southern, but I still do have great difficulty with the reasoning that keeps women always in the background, as if our minds and bodies were somehow less capable and active than theirs. That notion, however, is taught from birth, and I think they see no reason to change. If it was good enough for Dad, it is good enough for them.

Even my own sons, who certainly have been liberalized through no fault of their own, still maintain a bit of this macho mentality. By this I mean that to some degree women are treated as objects to be possessed rather than equal partners. I do think that Southern women perpetuate this concept in that they seem to love being flattered and touted about and ogled over. It puffs them up.

The older I became the more I felt like an object rather than a person. I bought into the system, hook, line, and sinker, at least until Martina came into my life.

I remember going to parties. Often they were small parties that included only the closest of our friends—all the young marrieds. Usually they were fun, but typically all the men converged in one part of the house, and the ladies, after addressing how "nice" each other looked, mingled among themselves with the usual chitchat.

I was often an exception at those parties because I had led an interesting life, traveled a bit, and early in marriage created a business in what was at the time a man's world. I was sometimes then accepted by the fellas on a different level from the other women and singled out to join in their conversations. I thought this a privilege until I realized that the other women became jealous of this extra attention. All along I was hoping that the attention was because of my mind. In the beginning I think it was, but as the evening progressed and the effects of the liquor set in, ultimately the attraction was to the body, not to the mind. It didn't seem to matter to the good ole boys whether I was married to one of their friends or not. In the end I was always the trophy to be won. That is not to say, however, that I was the *only* woman after whom they sought.

I remember always being uncomfortable with the advances of my husband's friends, even if the mentality of the advances was one of innocence. I was simply supposed to be flattered, or so said my husband when I would tell him of such attention and innuendos. He was proud that the other guys found *his* wife attractive, yet I was uncomfortable and demoralized. Would I ever live long enough to be appreciated by men and women alike for my mind and not for my looks? I say this not out of conceit nor out of any ungratefulness for my appearance.

I've always said that my best feature is my left foot and nobody ever pays much attention to it. That reminds me of a conversation I had with Howard Stern when I did an interview with him in 1995 on his radio-television show. He told me that his best features were his feet. He then took off his shoes and showed them to me. They were great feet, I'll have to admit. I just had never known anyone else who ever thought of his feet (or *foot*, in my case) as his best feature. We developed an immediate bond! It was like baring our soles, so to speak.

The advances of Southern men are not blatantly obvious. They are taught early on to always be gentlemen. It is not until the end of the evening when the goodbyes are being said that he sends his message loud and clear as he bends his head to kiss you good night (as is proper in the South). Instead of a whisper of a kiss upon the lips, it is an openmouthed kiss leaving nothing to question but the desire for privacy. After that message is sent, in the next chance meeting he will be much more verbally explicit. It is always done in a slightly jestful manner, just in case he is rejected. In my case, he always was.

The message was that I was supposed to feel flattered, but because I was married, I was safe. I did feel flattered. I did not feel safe. There always seemed to be a paradox in my life directly related to how I was taught versus how I felt.

An interesting question comes to mind now that I know I want to be with a woman: if a woman approached me in the same way as the men, would I feel scared? The answer is no, but I would feel uncomfortable. Does that mean that because a man is bigger and stronger that he invokes more fear, more threat of force? Yes, I guess it does. However, whether it were a man or a woman making the unsolicited advances, I would feel uncomfortable.

I think that Southern men have actually learned their lessons well. They do take care of their women. They *are* providers and they *are* attentive. I saw it in my grandfather. I saw it in my father and in my husband. I even see it to some degree in my sons. Perhaps only their sons will be rid of the "take care of" concept completely, at which point they should be able to enjoy a more equal marriage because their wives will know how to and will want to take care of themselves.

I think Southern men actually like women who are strong. They just do not want to admit it. If they truly think the strong part is not something they want in a woman, and that they want a woman who is entirely dependent, then they better have a closer look at their mothers!

I think the only lesson Southern men really need to be taught from birth is that ornaments are for Christmas trees.

# 4

## Maid of Cotton

On December 27, 1964, my life was changed. No, I did not discover that I was a lesbian. I was selected by a panel of judges in Memphis, Tennessee, to become the twenty-seventh National Maid of Cotton, the Southern girl's dream—just short of becoming Miss America! It happened much to my surprise. I reflect on it, and it still surprises me. I was not the prettiest and not even the smartest, but I had something they liked. I think it was a combination of things, not the least of which was that I had a lot of stamina. They concluded this from the many, many in-depth interviews each girl had with the judges over three days of judging. The Maid of Cotton always underwent a rigorous schedule during her year as the MOC, so being in good physical condition was essential. The tour lasted nine months, three of which were spent in foreign countries, the other six in the United States and Canada, and required being in two different cities each week. Every tenth day we would have three days for rest, then at it again.

I was nineteen when I was chosen, a student at Texas Christian University. The contest was held over our Christmas break. We were on a semester system and I had not taken my fall final exams when this happened. I remember calling all my professors at home very late that same evening to tell them the news, for I would not be returning home and exams would need to be delayed until the following August when I returned from the European tour. The tour was to begin the very next day, and my first official appearance was to be at the Cotton Bowl parade in downtown Dallas on January first. I was presented on the football field at halftime (Texas vs. Nebraska), then whisked away to the airport to fly directly to New York.

I do not ever remember being colder than I was that January 1, 1965, as I sat atop a beautiful float made out of cotton balls in a long, white, sleeveless evening gown (also of cotton!) waving to the gathered crowd, who were also freezing from the remains of a rare ice storm that had hit the area the night before. So if you see rigid smiles on the faces of girls on beautiful floats and arms that wave to the cheering crowds as if on mannequins, then have sympathy, for they may really be frozen, or perhaps just scared to death. The effect is the same.

Before I ever left Memphis, however, I was taken into the office of the president of the American Cotton Council. At that moment I became a woman of thirty, I think. I was told in no uncertain terms of my responsibilities as the Maid. A beauty queen I was not. The most important spokesperson for one of the largest industries in the world I was. I would be required not only to model an *all*-cotton wardrobe on runways across the country and the oceans for the next nine months, but I would have to speak at luncheons and banquets and dinners for dignitaries and royalty alike, do television and radio and newspaper interviews almost every day, and in general be an ambassador for the cotton industry throughout the world. I was nineteen. I was scared. I couldn't show it. I had to appear strong and self-assured. I had been groomed for this responsibility all my life, and I did not even know it. It was my first path out of the ordinary, but not my last.

I was chaperoned by two wonderful girls—real Southern ones. Sondra Otey, twenty-three, fresh out of college and from

Memphis, was the tour secretary. Patty Povall, twenty-seven, from Oxford, Mississippi, was the tour manager. Usually one or both positions were filled by a person who had previously been on the tour, a veteran so to speak. This year, none of us had ever been on the tour. We could do no wrong because we had no way of knowing what others had done before us. Often we just had to wing it. I will say that we were a pretty good team. Patty and Sondra were young, pretty, and charming, and often the officials who met our planes were confused as to which one of us was the real Maid of Cotton!

We were on a plane every third or fourth day traveling to some new destination, spreading the good news about the versatility of cotton. I had a wardrobe made for me by almost every leading designer in America and abroad. Bill Blass, Oleg Cassini, Adele Simpson, Geoffrey Beene, Halston, and Oscar de la Renta were just a few of the contributors. I was allowed to select shoes, handbags, and hats to go with each. It was a dream come true for this young, wide-eyed Texan. My clothes filled twenty-seven large suitcases, all of which went wherever I went. It would take two extra cars or taxis from the airports plus our limousine just to take the bags to the hotel. I got to keep all those clothes and all those suitcases. I have no idea where those dresses are now. I think my mother has saved a few for posterity. As a matter of fact, there is one for certain because I just wore it to a dance for lesbians in L.A. not long ago. I was the token prom queen. Never did I imagine in my wildest dreams that exactly thirty years after my Maid of Cotton reign, I would reign in one of my very same MOC formal dresses at an all-female affair where women could dance with other women and be happy and proud doing it. Life has provided me with some interesting choices.

A social life beyond the required daily events on the tour was difficult. There was simply no time. I missed my family terribly, although they were allowed to meet me for a few days during some of our rest stops. For the most part I was alone for the first time in my life. I had some growing up to do and I had to do it while no one was looking. I wrote letters and made calls to friends back home, but it just wasn't the same. A boyfriend or two would occasionally come to visit me in a scenic spot, but time and distance had put a strain on the relationships. They didn't last beyond that year. When I left for the contest in Memphis, I was dating boys my own age. When I returned to Fort Worth, I thought I had little or nothing in common with them and found myself much more comfortable with guys quite a bit older. This fact disturbed me. I didn't want to be all grown up yet. I had just spent a year being that and I really just wanted to be a little girl again. I missed that innocence. I wanted it back but couldn't turn back the pages. I was different. The world had changed me, I thought. In actuality I had changed my world.

I was asked to write a weekly column for the newspaper back home so that the whole town could keep up with their celebrity. I did. I really enjoyed it. It gave me a good reason to keep a diary of daily events, something I still do today. The discipline was and is a good one. It helps to freshen one's memory and jog the senses, which often have gone to sleep.

The next few pages are excerpts from my diary in 1965. They will perhaps, better than I can now, give some insights into that girl of nineteen who had to become a woman to the public.

*Saturday, April 17, 1965*

### Insights Into My Soul

I'll clue you in first off—I'm not in a very good mood right now. I guess it's because I can't seem to get along with Duncan very well—not that it's his fault, 'cause it's not—it's just the old Judy showing. I suppose the only boy that I have been completely in love with is Kurt, and I know that that would never work. Right now I don't know what will happen between Duncan and myself. This is our last night together so the next few hours will probably tell the tale. I'm the type of person that needs to feel like I'm wanted very much—guess I have some sort of complex about it, anyway I don't seem to get this satisfaction from Duncan—enough of that, just wait until tomorrow and get the final conclusion of the story. (Your guess is as good as mine.)

*Monday, April 19, 1965*

### Breakfast With Robert Mitchum

10:00 A.M.—Breakfast with <u>Robert Mitchum</u>!

I got up at 7:30—had fittings at Denver Dry Goods at 9:00. At 10:15 we got back to the hotel—I called Mr. Mitchum from my room—he came down and picked us up and we all went downstairs for breakfast. He was most delightful and attractive. He looks just like he does in the movies. We had some nice conversation. He had to leave at 11:00 for a radio interview then a luncheon at 12:30. At 2:30 was TV and then I met the mayor at 4:15. It was quite an exciting day. I wrote letters and then at 6:30 we went to Boulder with Sondra's friends for dinner. It was a lot of fun. I talked to the family tonight. I called Carol—I love her dearly and think she is the greatest. Bill Hurley called— nice talking to him.

*Friday, May 7, 1965*

### Today I Met the President of the United States

11:30 meet the President of the United States—Lyndon B. Johnson at the White House (first Maid of Cotton to ever get to do this).

TODAY I MET THE PRESIDENT OF THE UNITED STATES. It was the most exciting, wonderful, fabulous experience of my life. First I met Sec. of Agriculture Orville Freeman. Then I was taken to the White House to meet Lyndon B. Johnson. He was a majestic man. Looked very tired and like a man with much concern and a man who was concerned with the lives of people. We talked, laughed, and looked at the Rose Garden outside his office. He called in the press and within seconds hundreds of reporters— CBS, NBC, ABC, UPI—all were there watching, photographing as we talked. Afterwards I went into the Press Room and was asked by reporters as to what I had said and what he had said to me. I then went to a luncheon. Mrs. Jim Wright was there and also the wife of the Sec. of Health, Education, and Welfare. I modeled and spoke. Tonight I had dinner with Billie Sue Anderson, who is here for a few days. Talked to family.

### Thursday, July 1, 1965

### Adventure on My Travels

Today was such a fun day. We did exactly what we said that we would do when we got to Rome—we rode motor scooters! We got up at 11:10 A.M. (lazy). It was already very hot and almost time for all the shops to shut down until 4 P.M. We dressed, had our bread & tea, and walked to the place where we could rent motor scooters for $1.00 an hour. We rented them at 12:30 and finished at 3:30. It was hilarious! First they had a man show us how to operate the clutch, etc. After a few instructions we were on our way. Like idiots, I guess, 'cause the traffic in Rome is certainly not for the beginners! But we made it safely. (Got lost a few times.) We went to the Vatican City and saw St. Peter's cathedral—then rode around and, at last, found the Appian Way and out to the Catacombs. We just chanced upon it 'cause we were so lost! It was fun. My motor went dead a couple of times and I would have to get someone off the street to start it for me. Patty ran into the bushes while trying to turn around on a country road. We made our way back into town and then a young man drove ahead as we followed and showed us the way back to the place where we rented the scooters.

It always amazes me that people think that I went with Martina because she was rich and famous. That's really not saying much for Martina or me. I didn't know how much money she had. It didn't matter. I had been with rich boys and men all my life. If that's what I was looking for, I think it would have been easier on everyone had I married a wealthy man. And as for famous, in 1984 when I fell in love with Martina, she was well-known all right, but she wasn't exactly the most popular person in the world. Certainly not in my community. I had been with and around famous people long before Martina. Certainly the Maid of Cotton's public exposure afforded me that. I had breakfast with Robert Mitchum, lunch with James Garner, and talks and walks with Richard Chamberlain. I talked politics with Lyndon Johnson in the Oval Office and went sailing on the king of Spain's yacht. And so goes the tale. But little did I know then that I was the "fairy."

# 5

## Married: The Total Woman

It was December 16, 1967. I was twenty-two. I was walking
down the aisle of the First Methodist Church in downtown
Fort Worth, my arm entwined with my charming father's. My
dress was long and white and flowing. Tiny sequined beads
sewn on the dress made a pearl-like glow as I passed each of
the candles placed delicately along the long center aisle to the
front of the church. There at the altar I met my prince, or so
the story goes. My proud father gave my hand to my husband-
to-be. Eddie Nelson looked so handsome in his tails and white
gloves. He was also twenty-two. We were all grown up and
ready to take the vows that would bond us together for life, for
richer or poorer, in sickness and in health, till death did us part.
Little did we know that death would come seventeen years
later. Not a physical one, but an emotional one. Little did we
know that ten years into our marriage our heaven would become hell. Little did we know of the struggles that would force
us to grow. Little did we know that the fairy-tale world of Judy
and Ed would end in such an unbelievable way.

No one ever told us that our love might not withstand the
choices that would confront each of us. We were twenty-two.
Life was good. We were not told there would be surprises.

We were only taught that true love would endure all things. We were not taught about passages we would have to go through. We were not taught how to cope with our fears, for we had been told to be fearless. We were never informed that our marriage might be any less than perfect. We were not taught what to do if it was not. We were twenty-two.

That evening, in a church that overflowed with family and friends and guests, I took Ed's name. Judy Hill became Judy Nelson. I did not realize that I was giving up something, someone I had been all my life . . . Judy Hill. It was tradition. I accepted it. I did not question it. I would question it now. I would keep my name and add his to mine perhaps. Our own identity is one of the few things in life we can always keep. Knowing one's identity is one quest of life.

We entertained all the guests afterward at a grand and gala reception at the country club, then jetted off to Acapulco for a honeymoon at Las Brisas. As most newlyweds do, we saw a lot of the inside of our little cabana and very little of Acapulco. We were in love.

All too soon we had to return home. The local newspapers had run a story announcing our marriage. They made one big error, however. They printed our newly wedded names as Mr. and Mrs. Edward Hill. I remember how upset Ed's mother was about that. It set the tone for my relationship with my mother-in-law.

It was time to get on with our new life together. Ed went back to medical school where he was in his second semester of his first year. A long road lay ahead for him and for me. He would not be ready to go into private practice until our tenth year of marriage. I went back to teaching school. I taught an experimental course in speech and theater to second- and third-grade students in an underprivileged area of Dallas. One of the good things about it was that there was no set curriculum; I could design the course as I thought best. However, just about the time I would get the kids in their seats and quiet, a bell would ring and they would have to line up to march out to their next class. The bell drove me crazy. I hated its ringing to change classes every forty minutes. In theater one needs un-structured time with the students, and they were too young to be called back for rehearsals after school. Their attention span was short, anyway.

Besides all that I was newly married, rarely saw my hus-band, and missed my family. I disliked Dallas because I had never lived anyplace but Fort Worth, except for those couple of years when I was a kid. It was tough going. My paycheck was barely enough to buy groceries and pay the rent. Ed did not get a paycheck; he did have a partial scholarship. He was a really smart guy. Book smart that is. In life we both had a lot to learn.

Sex was good, although I didn't have a clue until I was twenty-seven about having a climax. I'm not sure even today how I figured out that I wasn't having one. Much to Ed's credit, however, the moment that I began asking him pertinent questions about what I was supposed to be feeling, he began to try to help me understand, and together we developed a new closeness in our pursuit of the ultimate bliss. He was wonder-fully patient, and when I did finally achieve an orgasm, I was astonished that I had lived happily all those years without one. I guess it's sort of like what you don't know won't hurt you. After that, lovemaking took on a whole new dimension, and the fulfillment added to the depth of our commitment.

After teaching school that first year of our marriage, I decided that my talents did not suit the challenge. I knew I had to find another way to support us. Thank God there are some wonderful and dedicated teachers out there. I just wasn't one of them. I desperately wanted to find something that would take us back to Fort Worth and my family. I didn't realize how con-nected I was to them—to the safety net that they provided. I wanted my safe and comfortable surroundings back again. I knew that Dallas was close enough that Ed could commute, for it was just thirty-five minutes away by the turnpike. Thus, if I could make enough money to justify the move, I was home free.

Already I was taking control. Funny because I was never taught about control. It was just one of those silent, unwritten laws that one does whatever one has to do to make things work, and that's what I thought I was doing. I did not know that my gallant efforts to make us a prosperous family with a wonderful house, in the perfect neighborhood, with two nice cars and two great kids who went to all the right preschools and prep schools, instead of just being like all the other poor medical-school families, would eventually be one of the things that would tear apart our Camelot. Even though in the years to come I made a lot of money, we lived beyond our means. This was my doing, not Ed's. He would have settled for much less, I think. He just never had the courage to stand up to me. Not until one night, only one month before he was finally going into private practice, he left. He made the only statement he had the courage to make, and that was simply to leave. The fairy tale was over.

Our lives would never be the same. I had worked hard to support a lifestyle to which we had no right at that point in our lives. Patience was not something I had learned. After teaching school, I sought and was approved for a license to open a franchise steak house, called Bonanza, that was popular during the late sixties and early seventies. I was the first woman licensee ever. I borrowed the money from my mother and a good friend of hers from Houston. I paid them back the first year. I drew a hefty salary for a woman in those times, and my steak house, located just blocks from TCU, where Ed and I had gone to college, was extremely successful. It was always among Bonanza's top ten in national sales each month. I was both proud and tired. I worked eighteen-hour days. I hired and fired, did the books, and cooked and cleaned when the help didn't show up for work. I would call in my parents to the rescue when some days I could not find enough good help to open shop or we had more business than we could keep up with and just needed more hands. They were always there for me. Always have been. There is something very extraordinary about a family you can say that about. Mine is.

I ran the restaurant even after Eddie, my first son, was born. I remember putting a playpen and a baby bed in my office in the back, just off the kitchen. There he would play or sleep. Either I or someone else would always be there to watch him and play with him. There I was being a liberated working mother and I didn't even know it. "I didn't even know it" would be a phrase that would come up more than once in my life.

When Ed left me that evening long ago, one of the reasons was that he was in love with another woman, and I didn't even know it.

When Ed left, our two sons, Eddie and Bales, were five and three years old, respectively. In 1970, the year before Eddie was born, I had a miscarriage five months into a pregnancy. That was physically one of the most painful experiences in my life. Emotionally it was devastating. Even now I find it hard to recapture those feelings. It's as if I've put them into a little box somewhere peaceful, never to be opened again. The feelings, however silent, add to my experience of life. I lived in fear until Eddie was born that I would never be able to have children, that something was physically wrong with me even though the doctors assured me otherwise. I did have a difficult delivery with Eddie, but he was healthy and he was ours. We were proud and happy parents. Two years and seven months later I had Bales, another healthy but very tiny baby. We now had two wonderful sons. We lived on an Indian reservation on the outskirts of Lawton, Oklahoma. Bales was one of only a few white babies born at that hospital. My father tells a funny story about sitting in the waiting room with all the expectant fathers while Ed was in the delivery area with me. All the expectant fathers were American Indians. Supposedly one had to be at least one-fourth Indian to be born in that hospital. My daddy said a very large Indian was sitting next to him and introduced himself as Chief something or other and asked Dad what tribe he was from! Daddy didn't know what to say except that he had to go right that minute. He hurriedly got up and asked to see Dr. Nelson so as not to have to answer any more "Indian" questions. Every time he told the story the chief got bigger and bigger! I do love Daddy's stories.

We lived across from the Indian hospital for two years. Ed joined the Public Health Service right after he finished his internship. The Vietnam War was winding down, but doctors were still being drafted. It seemed like a better idea to try to stay on U.S. soil, and we were lucky that they needed doctors on the reservation. Six or so other doctors and their wives were there, and we were all about the same age and all with budding families. I remember that we played a lot of bridge at each other's houses in the evenings while the kids all played together. I never liked bridge very much but Ed loved it. I would rather have been doing something active outdoors. It was, however, a good discipline for me. One evening while playing an intensely close game, my mind began to wander (a *big* mistake in bridge). I trumped Ed's ace. We played very few times after that unforgivable sin. I don't miss it at all. I don't even know if Ed still plays.

After our two-year stint in the Service, we moved back to Fort Worth. Most people I know were born, live, and die in that town. Ed started his own emergency-medicine practice and hated every moment of it. Ed was a thinker. He had to get back into medicine in a way that he felt most capable and comfortable. Emergency medicine was not the answer. Internal medicine was. After hours, days, and weeks of talking he decided to go back to Parkland Hospital in Dallas and do a residency in internal medicine. It would take him another two years. We already had eight years behind us and he still wasn't in private practice. It was a long, hard road. He was, and is, a dedicated doctor and probably the best internist in Fort Worth. I saw little of him the next couple of years. We had our home in Fort Worth, and he commuted back and forth to Dallas, a task that was difficult in itself. The drive, compounded by the burden of being a resident on call sometimes seventy-two hours at a time, was wearing on him, on me, and on his relationship with our two sons, with whom he never had the time nor the energy to play. He did find time and energy for something besides medicine. Her name was Julie.

Just a few weeks before our tenth anniversary and a month before Ed would finally go into private practice, he came into our bedroom late one afternoon and said that he had to leave. I asked him when he would be back, assuming that he had gotten a call to go to the hospital. He replied that he was not coming back, that he was leaving me. I was totally unaware. I would be caught unaware many more times in my life. With years of therapy under my belt I'm just now beginning to understand why.

The bubble had burst. The fairy tale had come to an end. I was never told that there would or could be an unhappy ending. I was always taught that if you were giving and caring and loving, things would always work out. They did not. I did not believe this was happening to me—a statement I have made time and again to my therapist, Annie Denver of Aspen, Colorado.

The pain was greater than any I had ever known. I didn't know where he had gone or where he was staying. My parents and family gathered around to comfort and protect me, but nothing, nothing eased the pain or diminished the loss. After a few days, with no word from him at all, I called his mother to see if she knew his whereabouts. She gave me a phone number of a motel room where he could be found temporarily. I called. He barely spoke. I cried. The end result was that he would come to the house to get some of his things and see the boys and we would try to talk. I had no information. I was clueless. It was a storm and I was far out to sea with the sails ripped away from the masts. I was sinking fast and I was frozen with fear. The only thoughts I had were, where had I failed him? Why would he even want to leave me? How had I not seen it coming?

I knew that I loved him and that I wanted him back for myself and for Eddie and Bales. I was willing to struggle with every fiber of my being to keep our marriage together. That's where I came from, that's how I was taught. I was not going to give up. I just didn't know where to start. Anger had not yet set in. Disbelief was the stage in which I was stuck. My mind was raging with thoughts. Perhaps there was another woman; but no, that just wasn't possible, I thought. Even if he didn't want me anymore, he surely didn't have time for anyone else. Yet I was obsessed with the thought, so I devised a way to try to get him to confess his sin. I didn't like bridge, but I was a damn good poker player, so I decided to call his bluff. I waited until he called again and asked to come by for more of his clothing. He was taking his time about moving them out, but had wasted no time in filing for a divorce. He had filed one week after he left. That blew me away. If I ever wondered if he was serious about leaving, that answered all my questions.

When he arrived, I asked if we could discuss our lives. It was obvious that he still was not ready to address real issues. Ed was like that. He would sit on the fence until someone pushed him off. I said without hesitation, "Who is she?" He said, "What do you mean?" I replied, "The girl I saw you with the other night when I came up behind you at a stoplight." He couldn't think quickly enough and fell for the bait, or maybe he just thought it was time to come clean. "Her name is Julie Winkle," he said. My heart was in my feet when I heard those words. There really was another woman. My God, what was I going to do? As best as I can recall, I was as I was taught to be. I was strong in his presence, then fell apart after he left. I must have cried for days or weeks. The pain was relentless and unwavering. There was no peace, no calm. I was certain I would never feel joy or happiness again.

I spoke with my preacher, the same one I would one day speak with again when I fell in love with Martina. I spoke with my childhood friend and current attorney, Jerry Loftin. I would speak with him again when Martina left me many years later. The advice from both was to keep communicating and to give Ed time. I did. For the next two years I lived through hell and lies and deceit. Ed and I met with each other in an odd and awkward sort of way. He had his Julie. I had me. I did not date, at least not until the end of those terrible two years during which Ed moved in and out of our house at least five different times. The pain of it was silent, like a cancer growing inside me. During my most desperate moments of despair and anger I created ways in which to trap him doing things with Julie, because he insisted that he was not seeing her. He swore that he was working on *our* relationship and just needed time to sort it all out.

He had, at least, sought the counsel of a good psychiatrist. I was allowed to meet with them only once or twice. I was told that this was all about Ed, not me. Boy, do I wish that *I* had gotten some help. Remember, I was taught to be strong. I was going to weather this storm alone. I had my family and I had some dear friends. I used those resources in times of complete and utter fear and despair.

To this day I have not told my family or sons the following story and have related it to only a few very close friends. I tell it now only to again break the code of silence with which I was taught to live. I borrowed a friend's car one evening and drove over to Ed's apartment before he arrived. I parked so as not to be seen. I waited. After about an hour, he drove up and walked up to his apartment. I waited. Ten minutes later, Julie Winkle drove up, parked her car beside his, opened her trunk, got out a small suitcase, and also walked up to Ed's apartment. I waited. Thirty minutes later they both came down, holding hands and smiling, and got into Ed's car and drove away. I followed. They parked outside a local movie theater. I even remember the movie: *Jaws*. I had already seen it and secretly wished that Ed would be eaten by the shark. If only this were a movie and not real life—especially my life. They bought tickets and disappeared inside. I waited. It was dark. I was furious. He had been lying about not seeing Julie, just as I had suspected.

I drove home. I got a large hammer and four of the biggest nails I could find. I went back to the theater parking lot. My heart was pounding. I felt like a criminal. But I was determined to do something awful. I did. I crawled on my hands and knees between the cars until I was beside his. I began as quietly as possible to hammer the four nails into each of his tires. I was certain I was going to get caught by some patrolling police car, but I was not thinking of the consequences of my act, only the act itself. I needed to be bad. I wanted to be bad. No more Jesus Judy. No more good Southern girl. All the tires went flat. I waited. I sat crunched over in the front seat of a borrowed car to wait and see the expression on his face when he found his car flat on the ground at midnight on a Saturday night. I waited. And then, I saw. Ed and Julie came out of the cinema and into the parking lot, to the car. I watched his shoulders slump. I relished the exasperated expression on his face as he tried to decide what to do. I didn't stay for the entire event. I waited only until help came from a service station down the road, then I went home to my lonely house. The boys had spent the night at Mother's. I was alone. I was bad. It almost felt good.

The affair with Julie went on for almost two years until I finally had enough. I called Jerry Loftin and told him that I was tired of Ed's sitting on the fence and that I was ready to cross-file for divorce. At this point, he agreed with me and began the proceedings. At least there was movement. I was taking back control of my life rather than letting Ed orchestrate this requiem of a slow death. Next I called Julie and asked to meet with her. She was at the same hospital as Ed, studying to be a physical therapist, I think. That is where they had met. I met her there, too, one afternoon. We went to a nearby cafe to talk. She was scared. I was scared. We talked frankly. We both loved the same man. How we must have fed his waning ego. The only thing we agreed on was that it was indeed time for him to make a choice.

He chose me, or so I was led to believe. With only one day left before we were to appear with our attorneys in court to have our divorce declared final, he called and asked if he could come home. I told him yes, with the condition that we renew our wedding vows at our church, by our preacher and with our sons present. He agreed. We did. We were a family again. Hopelessly in love we were not. We were going to struggle through the dirty waters of the affair for years to come.

One day, out of the blue, Julie called me. She had lost, so she wanted me to know that she wasn't his only affair. She said there had been at least four or five women before her. I told her I knew. I did not. My pride was at stake. Funny, I really didn't have much left, but I managed to handle that blow like a lady. I called Ed immediately at his office to relate the bewildering revelation. His only reaction was to thank me for handling the situation with grace and that we would discuss all of it later. There was no later. I was never allowed to talk about it or ask about those affairs. He had discussed it with his psychiatrist, and they had decided it was best left wrapped silently in its little package. I accepted this. Even today, the questions surrounding those affairs haunt me a bit. Mostly I wonder where he found the time. I guess those residents at the hospital are not as busy as they look on TV.

I decided to change. I would become the "total women"— the woman no man would ever want to leave. I bought the book hot off the press by Marabel Morgan, *The Total Woman*. It would be my bible. For the next year I sacrificed what little there was left of Judy Hill to become the woman with whom Ed Nelson could live: caring, loving, attentive, creative, and, above all, subservient and nonchallenging. He was the head of the house and I would not question his authority. He made the decisions. I lived with them. Or perhaps I died with them. While I was trying to achieve wifely perfection, Ed was still seeing Julie on the side. Again, I did not know. We were a year into our reconciliation when he called me into the bedroom and, with tears in his eyes, declared that he was supposed to leave me that evening. It was all planned. The only problem was he said he couldn't leave. He didn't know why, he just knew that he couldn't do it. With numb emotions I watched him almost pathetically. He was as confused a soul as I have ever seen. I was just about as pathetic because I told him that if he would call Julie in my presence and tell her that he would never see or talk to her again and that he truly loved me, then he could stay. He called her. He stayed with me. From that day forward my feeling for Ed began to slowly change. Something inside of me was dying. It was my passion.

I had taken up tennis during those years that Ed was coming and going. I needed to take out my frustrations on something, and that little yellow tennis ball was just about perfect. I played with intensity. I became pretty good, pretty quickly. I needed to focus on something other than my failing marriage. Tennis was the buffer. I kept on playing even after Ed came back home. One night at the dinner table, our son Eddie noted with a child's clarity that the only times I seemed happy were when I was playing tennis with my girlfriends at the club, and the moment that Ed came home I became somber. Those words rang truthfully in my ears for months to come. I went inside myself and had a good look at the person I had become. I didn't know her. I only liked that part of me that laughed with my girlfriends. I had regained my marriage, but I had given up my identity in an effort to please Ed.

Ed had first left when I was thirty-two. I was now thirty-seven, almost thirty-eight. It had been a long, hard struggle, and in the end I had nothing left to give. I had lost me. I wrote Ed a card and mailed it to his office. It said that I did not think I was in love with him anymore and that I was scared. A week passed and he still did not respond to my distraught message. Finally I asked him if he had received the card. He thought for a moment, then replied that he had and had intended to call me when he read it, but had gotten busy at the office and had forgotten all about it. He apologized and said simply that he truly loved me now, and that if I was having some problems, then they were mine to deal with. He was fine; I was not.

I wish I had had the courage to tell Ed after I found out about Julie Winkle and his other infidelities that either we should seek marriage counseling or therapy together or I would leave. I should never have remained in a relationship where I felt I had to sacrifice my identity for the sake of the marriage. But I was never taught that I had other options. In the end, was that sacrifice that drained my heart of all love and emotion for him.

Three months after I wrote Ed the card, Martina called me at home. We had spoken by phone a few times since our first meeting in 1982 and had exchanged Christmas cards, but we had not seen each other since then. She said she was going to be in Dallas in just a few days and would love to get together. She suggested that I meet her and watch one of her practices. I did. A new love story began. This time it was mine.

My wedding picture. Ed Nelson is at right with his arm around my mother.

With Martina in other times

rtina applauding my tennis form in England before Wimbledon

With my sister, Jan, Gloria Burdette, Martina, Frank Albero, and my mother at the gala debut for the MN clothing line at the Plaza hotel

One of my favorite photographs

COURTESY JEFF BARK

With Rita Mae Brown getting ready before a polo game

With Rita Mae and Gloria Steinem

In polo action in Virginia

Kay and Lauren
in front of Kay's
Paris apartment

With Kay and our dogs in Nellysford, Virginia

Kay in the Dodge Ram pickup with Nellie

# 6

## Married With Children

I think Ed would agree that the most important part of our union was that it produced two very special people, Eddie and Bales. I have a special bond with my sons. My choices in life have not been easy for them, but perhaps because of those choices we have all become stronger and closer. At times it was all we could do to just hold each other and cry to bear the pain. We were a threesome all their young lives because Ed was always at the hospital or just gone completely. We are a threesome now that they are all grown up. We have and have always had a unique and open relationship.

Eddie was given the name of his father, Edward Reese Nelson, and that made him the third. He was born in 1971, in Fort Worth at the same hospital where I was born. He weighed seven pounds and eleven ounces, which was a bit too big for my narrow pelvis. We learned that only after a difficult delivery. Apparently he got stuck in the birth canal and was facedown instead of faceup. The doctor had to use forceps on his head to both pull and rotate him 180 degrees. Out he came after some trauma and distress. I was totally unconscious and unaware of any of this until the next morning. Then, my pediatrician came by my room and said that he hadn't realized that I had already had the baby. He offered to go have a look at him and come back and give me a full report, as I had not yet seen my baby or Ed or my obstetrician. He returned a few minutes later, and assuming I would understand since I was a medical student's wife, said that Eddie was fine, but that he had a little torticollis, was jaundiced, and had a cephalhematoma. That didn't sound fine to me! I was petrified and tried not to show it.

I hastily asked the nurse to page my husband for me. When Ed appeared about ten minutes later, I asked him to explain Eddie's condition. He said that torticollis was the result of having to turn the head with the forceps, causing the muscles in the neck to spasm, and therefore the head was twisted to one side. The jaundice was a result of a loss of blood due to the cephalhematoma, making him appear yellow. The cephalhematoma was a blood clot on the top of his head, the result of a skull fracture caused by the force of the forceps. Ed and all the doctors assured me that all these things were temporary and not serious.

It didn't matter what they said, I was afraid. When the nurse finally brought Eddie in to me, he was indeed yellow and had a twisted neck and a lump on the top of his tiny head that was larger than an egg. He looked somewhat like a conehead. He could have been a baby from another planet, but he was mine and I thought he was the most beautiful baby I had ever seen! All the symptoms did clear up, although it took almost a year for the knot on his head to go away.

Bales was my second son. He was born in 1973 in Lawton, Oklahoma. He was given the maiden names of both our mothers, Bales Woodall Nelson. He was tiny. He weighed just five and a half pounds due to being delivered three weeks early. Labor was actually induced to try for a smaller baby, one that I could deliver more easily. When they handed him to me, I held him in the palm of one hand. He was like a little monkey. He was so small that I was afraid all over again. He grew fast, though. He gained the weight that he needed and was a bundle of activity.

Now with two fine sons, I was a proud and happy mother. We did everything together. I didn't have any help, except for family, so I always took my sons everywhere I went. Because of this they were well-adjusted and behaved. They were comfortable in almost every situation and seemed to know inherently what was expected of them.

They were athletic little guys, always playing every sport. They still do. I taught them how to play the sports that I could, and they had lessons in all the others. I often volunteered to be a coach for one of their teams if one was needed. I was usually the only mother who did that. Back in those days, most mothers just watched while the fathers coached.

Eddie always said that he would be president of the United States or else a professional athlete of some kind. Bales on the other hand wanted to create movies—direct, produce, or act in them. If that didn't happen, then he, too, would be a professional athlete.

Today Eddie is in his last year of law school. He professes that he can never be president because his mother is a lesbian. I'm sure Newt would agree with him. At any rate, he'll stay in Fort Worth—probably live and die there. Bales is in his last year as an undergraduate, majoring in television and film. I expect he'll eventually go to California and see what he can create. He'll be great—I feel it. Maybe he will eventually get back to Fort Worth, but I don't think that is as important to him.

Eddie was always a precocious child. He was a thinker. I remember after Ed left me, he came back to pick up some of his things. He told me that he had called Eddie into his office at the house and had tried to explain to him what had happened to our marriage, and why he had to leave. I wish I had been in there for that explanation, for perhaps it would have given me some insights. Ed said Eddie sat calmly in a chair across from his with his little hands on his chin. He was only five. He was silent as he listened intently. After Ed had spoken, he paused for a moment, and then he said Eddie looked straight at him with those blue, blue eyes and simply said, "Well, Dad, I don't know what to tell you. I think you've done everything you can." Ed said it was as if Eddie thought that he was being asked for advice. Ed said they both just sat for a moment looking at each other, and then Ed broke the silence by saying, "Thank you, Eddie," They never discussed our separation again to my knowledge, at least not when the boys were young.

Bales was just three when Ed first left me. When he was twenty, he went to a therapist who had counseled all of us at one time or another after I had gone with Martina. Bales was experiencing some depression with my move to Virginia and Eddie's move to Austin for law school. He was feeling abandoned. Because of this, the issue of Ed's leaving when Bales was a small boy came up. The therapist, a wonderful lady and friend, Dorothy St. John, knew the family history well and asked Bales to recall how he felt when Ed left. Bales later called to tell me that he could not answer her question because he had no recollection of Ed's leaving, even though he knew it had happened. Bales had blocked out all those feelings for all his life. I was amazed.

It is always interesting, and sometimes comical, when we as parents hear stories of our children's perceptions of us, especially when they are young. Eddie's kindergarten teacher told me Eddie was asked what his father did for a living. He said, "He is a doctor." The teacher then asked him what his mother did. Without hesitation Eddie replied, "She drives a car." As always, he was right on the money! It seemed as if that is all I did when they were young. I'm certain that mothers around America can relate to the simple truth of that observation. All I know is that I prayed for the day when they could have their own driver's licenses. And once they did, I prayed that they would live and that I would live through it. We all did, but not without crashes and bumps and lots of insurance claims. Eddie drives without any thoughts of actually driving; Bales drives as if he were Mario Andretti. Both have a guardian angel, I'm sure.

My relationship with my sons was always exceptional—a little out of the ordinary. Perhaps it was because of all we went through together, or perhaps it was because I always taught them that they could come to me with anything, no matter what—good or bad. I always told them that I would never, ever punish them for telling me the truth, whether I agreed with it or not, and I never veered from my promise. It was a trade-off that paid off. They felt that they could tell me anything and everything. They sure did.

I'll never forget the time that I was at home in Fort Worth spending some much needed time with Eddie and Bales. Martina had gone to play an exhibition match against Chris Evert. Eddie and Bales were throwing a "Tigua" party (named after their love of the island of Antigua in the British West Indies) at their dad's house. Ed was out of town for the weekend, but Eddie was old enough to be in charge. Eddie was a most responsible guy. He was always the kind of youth that mothers and dads loved for their daughters to date. Solid. Anyway, about 11 P.M. Bales phoned to tell me that one of the younger boys had passed out from too much alcohol. They couldn't get him to come to and were really scared. Bales said he knew I was the only mom that they could call who would know what to do and not panic or reprimand them on the spot for such forbidden behavior. As it turned out, the boy would have died from too much alcohol in the blood had they not called me. I told them to get an ambulance and meet me at the emergency room. They did. (Eddie stayed at the house to continue chaperoning.) The boy's life was saved, but only by a matter of minutes, the doctors told us.

I talked to Bales and his friends who had come to the hospital, and we discussed the severity of the situation. I asked each boy to talk with the doctor so they could learn something from the almost fatal incident. In the meantime I called the young boy's parents, whom I did not know. Bales took some leadership again and spoke with the parents, representing all the kids. He was very brave, and I was proud that he took responsibility under such critical circumstances. Most of all I was grateful that Bales and I had a trusting relationship. I hold that story near and dear to my heart because I think it says so much about the kind of open and honest relationship we have always shared. I love that.

The years spent with Eddie and Bales growing up would be filled with unforgettable stories of loss and love, of failure and victory, of boredom and adventure, of disbelief and belief, and of stagnation and change. I put these stories on the pages in my heart that are reserved for Eddie and Bales only. They write upon those pages still. I suppose they always will. That's part of the beauty of being a mother.

As much as I only wanted to give them a beautiful and perfect world, I could not. It is said that only from pain do we grow. We grew. Their first pain was the pain of Ed's leaving when they were so young. Then it was the pain and devastation of my leaving Ed and falling in love with a woman. That was in 1984. At the time none of us knew if we would ever be a family again. We did know that we would never be the same and that life as we knew it had changed forever.

I remember their anguish and tears and fears. The immediate focus was not on my going to live with a woman, but on their parents' getting a divorce. Later, when they realized that the divorce was inevitable, the focus was on my having chosen a woman for my life partner. I'll never forget Eddie's anger with that thought. He was just twelve and only beginning to have a real look at his own sexuality. I was turning his world upside down. Neither he nor anyone else in my family had any experience in such matters. We didn't even know any lesbians. For all they knew I was the only "heterosexual lesbian" in the world—certainly a contradiction in terms, but they just couldn't believe that I, their mother, was a lesbian. To some degree, my family still doesn't. It has been several years since Martina left, and yes, I'm in love with a woman again. But that's another story.

The fact remains that at age twelve Eddie's perfect world had crumbled once more and he was mad as hell. In one of our therapy sessions with Dorothy St. John, he put it bluntly and boldly: "I'm angry because you [meaning me] changed my life forever. It will never be as I planned it. And I can't do anything about it." Those words would haunt my nights for months and years to come. Only when he became eighteen was I relieved of some of the guilt I felt, when he spontaneously came to Martina and me and said, as we all sat in a limousine that was taking us to a pro-celebrity event in Florida, "You know, I told you once that I was so angry because you had changed my life forever. I realize now that you changed it for the *better*. I am a better person for having gone through all that I have." And he said, "Martina, I'm better physically because of you. You forced me to be better than I would have been otherwise, because you just can't be a guy and be a wimp around you." We were amazed at his candor. I took those words and put them away in that little box I have reserved for Eddie and Bales in my heart. They warm me on nights when I am filled with cold despair and sadness for the pain I have caused others to suffer on my behalf. But I have followed my heart. And I always will.

It was also in a therapy session with Dorothy that Eddie and Bales asked a big question for two young boys plagued by the fact that their mother was living with a woman. They wanted to know what she was to them. If she wasn't their mother, and she wasn't their father, then what was she? Dorothy's calm reply was that she simply was their friend. She had been their friend before they knew we were going to be together, and she could simply remain that. She did. The relationship from that day forward changed for the better.

Even though our marriage did not last, I think Ed and I deserve a pat on the back for the way we handled our divorce with our sons. We agreed on joint responsibilities as far as they were concerned. We have shared equally in their upbringing and education both emotionally and financially. That was by choice, not by demand of the court. We never had designated days or holidays or vacation times or even homes. The boys were completely free to establish their own schedules and could move between both homes, as we lived only five minutes apart, according to their own comfort. They never had to pack suitcases to see one or the other of us as they had belongings in both homes. Even their friends seemed to adapt to the situation and simply referred to visits as at Judy's house or Ed's house. Ed and I were good at agreeing on any discipline or direction for the boys. We mostly talked by phone, but from time to time would have little "family meetings." I think because of their ages, reflecting their emotional needs, Bales (being nine at the time of the divorce) spent most of his time with me, while Eddie (twelve) chose to spend most of his time at Ed's. Bales still needed "Mother" and Eddie was moving into another stage where the relationship with "Dad" would become more important. This was as it should be and we understood it. We didn't get our feelings hurt.

Actually Ed and I probably related better after the divorce because we had only to focus on raising our sons and not on *our* relationship. We are still friends today. That is not to say that he wasn't devastated when I went with Martina. He was. He was angry beyond belief and made statements to the effect that I would never see my sons again. He hated Martina, but he didn't hate me. After the fire and smoke disappeared and each of us could see more clearly, we knew that we had to put personal feelings aside and concentrate our energy on what was best for our children. Today, we do not talk much because the boys are grown and our lives have taken such different paths. Ed has long since remarried, not to Julie but to another nurse.

They have started a new family of their own—one young son and a new baby girl. I am with a woman. It is my choice.

When I left Ed, I was told that he gave my relationship with Martina six months, then a year, then two. I heard that after five years he said that he thought I was truly happy and that perhaps it would last a lifetime. It did not. I, too, expected it to last forever, but then I had expected my marriage with Ed to last a lifetime.

We all came a long way during those years I was with Martina. Eddie and Bales and I had to learn a new way to relate. We had a new family structure, one with uncharted disciplines. There were no rules, no role models, for such a family unit: one mother, one very famous tennis player, and two young sons. My parents came to the rescue, something they continue to do even now, for all of us They sold their home and moved into our home. As I had to be on the road week after week, tournament after tournament, they maintained the household. They carpooled the kids, attended whatever school function I had to miss, made certain Eddie and Bales had done their homework, and provided the stability the boys needed when I so often had to be away Monday through Friday. On the weekends one or both boys, and many times a friend of each, would hop on a plane and meet us wherever the tennis tournament was being played. This looked glamorous to every observer, but to each of us it was a tiring and difficult way to live. We made it work. Much to Martina's credit, she was very supportive and knew that it was the only way I could travel with her each week. We talked about this lifestyle and jet-set kind of schedule before we were committed to each other. I was a mother with two sons. Her needs would become my responsibility, but so were my sons. I just had to find a way to make it all work. It was a balancing act, and in retrospect I wonder how I made it without falling. In retrospect, perhaps I did.

We even had to create ways to do homework together: check, countercheck, just as we had always done. That is when

I discovered the fax machine. We became a futuristic "family by fax." I would receive papers and essays by fax. I would then make corrections or suggestions, and often we would phone each other to discuss the homework as each of us held a copy. It worked. Their grades never seemed to suffer. Incentive waxed and waned because of the unusual pressures and struggles created by such a lifestyle, but we always kept the communication open. Most important, there was an abundance of love.

I could not have made this unusual family structure work if it had not been for the endless work, love, and support from my parents. They became surrogate parents from Monday to Friday. They never complained. They loved unconditionally and worked tirelessly and endlessly.

Martina gained Eddie's and Bales's respect. They later began to be proud to have her around them. I remember at Eddie's sports awards banquet his senior year, he was to receive some special recognition for his achievements, and he proudly had Martina and me there as a couple to watch him. We even sat at the dinner table beside Dr. Ed and his new wife. We had "come a long way, baby."

Eddie went to college. Bales was entering his senior year in high school and Martina and I had planned that at that time we would move to Aspen, Colorado. It would become our main and permanent residence. All along Bales had said that he would make the move with us. He changed his mind. He decided, and rightly so, that he wanted to graduate with the friends he had gone to school with since kindergarten. Although I was more upset about his decision than I allowed anyone to see, it was his choice and not mine. He decided to stay in Fort Worth with Ed and would come to Aspen to be with us as soon as school was out. He would also spend many weekends and all vacation time with us. This compromise was internally tearing me apart. The move to Aspen had been planned for a long time, and there was no turning back at that late date. Bales would have to understand. I don't think he ever did. I rationalized it: because we had to be gone most of the time anyway, not much had changed except our residence. Or so I thought.

A lot had changed. Martina and I broke up that same year. The house we were building would be left incomplete for two years while she declared what to do with her new life. Life without Judy. Judy without Martina. Eddie and Bales without their friend. She had over the past seven and a half years become a parentlike figure to both of them. There was a loss. Again, life would be forever changed.

I remained in Aspen alone in a house that later became mine. Martina moved to a small house that we had purchased after our first visit together to Aspen, some seven years prior. I really didn't know if she would stay in Aspen or not. I knew that I couldn't afford it. I stayed for a year and a half until just after we came up with a settlement agreement out of court that made the front pages of all the scandal magazines and newspapers everywhere. Eddie and Bales were my support system, and they took care of me. For as long as they could, they put aside their own emotions in an effort to be strong for me. They could not maintain that strength forever, for they were hurting, too. We had been family—a unique one, an unusual one, but a *real* one.

Eddie and Bales and I created a new and even stronger bond. We spent as much time as possible together. The laughter we had known was slow in returning. It did return, but the sound of it had a hollowness. Today we can speak freely of those days and years with Martina, but even still there is sometimes a slight glisten of a tear in the eye of one or the other of them, not out of sadness, but because we remember the courage it took to be a family in the face of a world that didn't understand or accept it. We learned, and we grew.

# 7

## Eddie and Bales:
## Their Own Voices

### EDDIE SPEAKS

I believe I was twelve years old when my parents parted ways for the last time. I had not seen the split coming. I was angry and confused. Actually, I felt as if everything were running along smoothly, as if we were destined to be a happy family again.

As so often is the case, however, parents shield their children from their grumbling and discord. Bales and I were shipped off to our summer camp, worry free. What we knew was that Mom had a new best friend, courtesy of my introduction, and that she was to travel through Europe for a few weeks and perhaps catch a match or two. How could Mom resist such an invitation? Anyway, she would be home in time to pick us up from camp.

On that last day of camp, on a seemingly long drive home, Mom and Dad informed Bales and me that Mom would soon resume her stint abroad, at Wimbledon no less, and that they would soon divorce. My steady stream of tears didn't stop, they only merged with rage. Internally, despite an inkling of Dad's past marital transgressions, I began to construct an emotional wall at Mom's feet. This time, it was her fault.

I still hadn't put two and two together so to speak with respect to Mom's newfound sexual orientation, and I didn't for months. But my suspicions began to mount, and when confirmed, the mortar on that completed wall dried. Martina stole my mom, stole her heart, but without my permission.

Securely entrenched on my father's side, I was forced to grow up quickly. Given Martina's worldwide popularity, or notoriety in some cases, the press wet its figurative pants over such an intriguing opportunity to delve into the story behind Martina's latest acquisition. Bales and I were hounded for several weeks wherever we went. Fat, pale Englishmen hid behind trees to snap pictures of us playing in the front yard of my dad's house. Dad turned overzealous tabloid reporters away at the door daily.

Bales grew fond of Martina soon after she bought a house on the Shady Oaks Country Club golf course in Fort Worth. He was either too young to grasp the nature of Mom's relationship with Martina or too young to care. He only knew that where Mom was, he wanted to be. When Mom was in town, Bales lived with her. I lived with Dad full-time. It was my way of ignoring Mom's new way of life and punishing her at the same time.

I eventually warmed to Martina as we had so much in common, namely athletics. I grew to love her as my friend, although I remained opposed to the homosexual component of the relationship. I suppose that since Mom and Martina kept any physical sexual action rather covert, it was either for me to accept Martina and to accept the relationship.

Surprisingly, I never lost a friend as a result of Mom's homosexuality, and no one ever attempted to insult me directly. I guess I had, and still have, some true friends who never judged me or ostracized me for what they must, at least initially, have perceived as a shockingly improper choice by my mom. In fact, most, if not all, of my friends (including girlfriends) grew attached to or comfortable with Martina. She was magnetic. I loved Martina and I believed that the bond between Martina and Mom would last an eternity.

In retrospect, I gained so much during the seven years that Martina was a part of my life. Besides gaining an appreciation for health and fitness, I became even more competitive than I was already. I worked harder to be better at everything. More importantly, I grew close to my brother. Growing up, Bales and I fought often as so many siblings close in age do. Perhaps this is simply a consequence of living with each other day in and day out; however, we were afforded a unique opportunity to live apart almost half of the time yet still see each other virtually every day. Mom and Martina's house in Fort Worth was a mere five-minute bicycle ride from Dad's house. Until I could drive, I would simply pedal over to Mom's after school (when she was in town) and return to Dad's at night. This pre–high school ritual created some breathing room for both Bales and me. Consequently, we didn't get on each other's nerves so often, and today, we are the best of friends. That will never change.

Mom and I are the best of friends as well. Even though I don't see her enough, we speak every day. I do worry about her. She is a strong-willed, independently minded woman and can handle herself. She has been through substantial unwarranted adversity since Martina left. No one will ever know the scope of Mom's dedication and hard work in Martina's shadow. Mom made everything work and took little time just for herself. Traveling with Martina wasn't all glitz and glamour. In my heart, I know that Mom will find her niche in life. Good things happen to good people.

## BALES SPEAKS

Life can change in an instant. All the dreams that you have can be transformed overnight. This is not any great revelation, because every person learns to deal with life. But what do you do when the changes that you have to face are not your fault? When we are children, we learn to rely on our parents—we must. It is their duty to see that we are safe. A typical family follows certain guidelines. There is the mother, the father, an older and a younger. Everything is great, and "father knows best." However, life can not always fit the norm and we must make our own rules to play the game. My family has had to learn to play by their own rules.

I know that this story is getting old, but here it is briefly, one last time. When I was a child, my parents were divorced. No big deal—it is an easy out in today's society. But my parents' divorce had a twist. Most kids inherit a new mother and father. My brother and I were so lucky as to receive two mothers. In others words, my mother had chosen to live with another woman. So, life goes on, right? Not when your mother chooses to become the companion of a celebrity athlete. The whole world would shortly realize that my mother was gay. I was too young to care. I needed my mother and she, of course, needed me. (She always has and always will.) My brother, on the other hand, was three years older and was not receptive to his new surroundings. To make an incredibly long story short, my mom was with a woman, my dad was with a woman, and my brother and I were left to deal with this in our own way.

Looking back on the whole thing now, I realize that many different things were affected in my life. My stand on homosexuality is simple. DON'T DO IT! (I'm just kidding—thought that would raise an eyebrow or two.) I really don't understand that word. Sure, I understand that it means that people of the same gender prefer one another. But why do we have to label such feelings? I do not agree with homosexuality, but, as well, I do not judge anybody. Gay or straight, one is a human being. We all have feelings, desires, and goals. There is no difference. People are people.

Anyway, back to my life. Many things did change for me. I decided to live with my mother and her friend. It was a unique situation. They were gone for six months out of the year. I missed them both very much, but it was a great opportunity for me to get to know my dad. He and I were not close when I was a kid; actually he kind of scared me. I think that he came from the school of thought that if you scare the shit out of your children, then they will perform. Thank God he grew out of that stage. Actually we grew out of it together. He is a great man and the smartest I know. Every person makes mistakes, and that is okay. We forgive, forget, and go on. Dad and I are great friends. We have had our ups and downs, but I wouldn't change him for anything.

My mother is a different story. She and I have always been close. To call her my friend is an understatement. She keeps me going and she keeps me sane. She is a wonderful person whom I admire for her courage. She left us to be with another woman, but knew that in time we would somehow follow. She has never let us down. She stands strong for what she believes in, and that gives her credibility. Because of the lady that she is and her class, my views on life have changed for the better.

That brings me to my brother. I guess I should start by saying that I used to hate him. In my eyes he had chosen to distance himself from me and Mom in the beginning. That really hurt my mother. I had an English teacher in the sixth grade who used to tell me that if you cared enough to hate someone, then you must really love them. I don't have a clue in the world as to what that means, but I guess it is true. I never really hated my brother, and I know he is my best friend. We learned to deal with adversity together. We have the same views about many things and disagree on the same amount. Our relationship is very balanced, and for the most part, it is a wonderful friendship. We do still have some brotherly quarrels, though. All in all, we are there for each other. No one else in this world can comprehend what he and I have endured. And when times get rough, when no one else can truly understand my hurt, my big brother is always there.

That covers the three other people in my family and where they all stand in their relationships with me. But I suppose that I will end by telling you where my life is now. I am a senior at Texas Christian University, or will be by the time this gets out. My life has changed a lot since the day my mom decided to go with another woman. The first woman was special to me and it hurts for me even to talk about her. We accepted her into our family as one of our own. We loved her and devoted our lives to the bond that she shared with Mom. But life is just a game to her, and no matter how smart she thinks she is, she does not know how to play it. Life is one game that she has lost at "love." We have moved on from those days and our lives have more meaning. My mom was involved with another woman. I think they were better as friends and realized it. Now I think she has met her final companion, and that makes me happy. This woman is very caring and fits into our family just fine.

My brother is about to graduate from law school and I am very proud of him. Through all that we have been through, he charted the straightest course. My dad is still defying his age and has been given a wonderful friend in his wife. They have, together, given us a new brother and sister. As for me, I look forward to finishing college and making my own mark on this world. I have a lot to say and many things to express. Someday the world will learn to accept people for who they are inside, and not for the choices that they make in their personal lives. My mom made her choice to live her life with a woman. She is happy. Enough said.

# 8

## Martina: Nine Is More Than Enough

And there was this woman. I fell in love with her, happily, help-lessly in love with her. Wouldn't it be easy if that's all that needed to be said about my seven-and-a-half-year relationship with Martina? For me, that says it all—no questions, just the intense, wonderful feelings that being truly in love brings to a person.

After a few months of speculation, our relationship was accepted wholeheartedly by the lesbian community. I, however, was exiled from the heterosexual one that I had grown up in and to which I had given all my energy and sometimes my talents. The heterosexuals had no need for a newly emerged lesbian, no matter what her contributions. In that community I had fallen from grace, and it was determined that I was either sick or middle-aged crazy or perhaps both. Those who loved me did so in spite of controversy and disbelief. Those few family and friends became my backbone. They held me up when often all I could do was stumble. Their unconditional love has remained my strength. When Martina left me, I again became the fallen angel, only this time in the lesbian community as well as most of the heterosexual society. My only support came from the whispers of persons whose names and faces would never be seen or quoted.

One should never dare to go up against an icon. It is a fate close to death. I died at least a thousand lives. In the end, my family was judged and ridiculed as well. That fact was at times more than I could bear. But from the pain I have grown to know myself better. I now, at last, with more clarity, can address the issues involved in that love affair.

Life is not as simple as I would have it be. It is usually only in retrospect that we have any real understanding of our paths and our choices. Thus, I give you my reflections.

It was my path. I had not seen it coming. In 1982 I met this special woman. My older son, Eddie, introduced us. In retrospect I think he has many mixed feelings about that, for even though he eventually grew to love Martina, my falling in love with her was certainly not included in the perfect picture of how he thought his life would be painted.

The introduction was brief, but an instant bond was forged. She would be in my life and I in hers. But at that moment, in 1982, at the Bridgestone World's Doubles Championship held in Fort Worth that year, and only that year, neither of us was aware just how our lives would ultimately fit together. Neither of us knew at that brief meeting that only two years later we would meet again and fall deeply in love, so deeply that I would feel compelled to follow my heart to find my true self. Little did I know that I would be willing to risk everything in my life to live with this woman most of the world knew simply as Martina.

She left town immediately following that tournament (which she and Pam Shriver won), but not without giving me her mailing address. I gave her mine, as well as my phone number. We agreed it would be nice to keep in touch, as her home base at that time was Dallas and that was only a thirty-minute drive from Fort Worth.

We did not see each other for two years. That was fate, I suppose, for had she come into my life any earlier, I do not think I would have been ready for any romantic involvement: I was still bound and determined to try to hold my marriage together. When Martina reappeared in my life in 1984, I was open and ready for love in my life. I was no longer in love with my husband. I felt dead inside. Martina gave my heart new life, new hope. I was fearfully amazed that it was a woman who could fill my empty heart, but the fear was overcome by the feelings of love and passion. My fear was not for myself; it was for my family. I was joyfully ecstatic, yet my family felt only pain and confusion. My only times of apprehension came when I would sit and talk and try to explain my feelings to them, and I would see in their eyes the sorrow and the tears that my choice had caused. For that I was profoundly sad. My greatest challenge would be to show them how wonderfully happy I was with this woman and hope that that would ultimately change their minds and hearts. It did.

Between 1982 and 1984 Martina and I tried to get together once when she was going to be in Dallas for the Virginia Slims Tennis Tournament, but couldn't because I was going away with my family to ski. In March 1984 she called to see if I would be in town during the Slims Tournament. I was. She invited me to watch her practice the day before the tournament.

I went. She injured her hamstring, and the practice was cut short. Because of that we had time for a late lunch before I had to be back home. Only a few tables were occupied in the small, lovely hotel restaurant, as it was midafternoon and the business crowd had already gone back to work. These were our first moments alone. We spent several hours barely eating our soups and sandwiches, as there seemed to be so much to say. At that lunch, a past lifetime was shared and a new lifetime was begun. We fell in love over chicken-salad sandwiches and iced tea. It could have been caviar and champagne, and I would not have noticed the difference. My lonely heart was awakened by a woman instead of a man, and it just didn't matter. I wanted to know this woman in a way that I had never wanted to know any other woman in my life. It was not about whether this was a man or a woman. It was about being in love. The feeling was the same. And I could tell the feeling was mutual.

The next weeks were spent almost exclusively together, at least as much of the day as I could afford. The nights still belonged to my family. I missed her those evenings. I wished that I could have spent them with her instead. I hoped and believed that perhaps one day I would spend my nights, too, with her.

Then there was the first kiss. I have to admit that, far from my good-Southern-girl upbringing, I was the aggressor. Martina opened the door a crack, and I boldly pushed it open all the way and walked right in. We had gone to the house of a friend of Martina's to have some time alone to talk, as we were still just getting to know each other. After about an hour we knew that we had to get back to the tennis tournament, where we had originally been watching matches—stealing precious time together. Just before we were leaving, she turned to me and said, "Well, what do you want to do?" I knew the unspoken message behind the question, and I replied, "I think I want to kiss you." With no hesitation and without another word, we kissed. It was soft and warm and sensual. I knew at that moment there would be thousands of kisses to come. It was a first kiss. It was a kiss that said what no words could say. My heart at long last had found its home.

We fell in love. It did not matter to me that she was famous. It would perhaps have been simpler had she not been so visible. For, as it was, we were to stand in judgment of a heterosexual world and in awe of a lesbian community. Even acceptance from the latter would come only after the skepticism was put to rest, and that would take time, lots of time. If I was going to be the lover and partner of the gay community's hero, I had to prove myself worthy. That in and of itself was no easy task. I was to follow in the footsteps of some very famous and powerful lovers of Martina's. I did not know of these ladies at the time, nor did I care about her previous relationships. All I knew and all I wanted to know was that *I* was her love. I thought I was to be her greatest love, and her last. I was not. But to this date I was her longest; I would like to think also her best and happiest. We must have done something right, for seven years is no mere itch.

During those years she was the number one tennis player in the world. All eyes were on this remarkable athlete, analyzing her tennis and her private life. She gave women of the world, as well as men, a standard by which to be judged. She created a whole new level of physical fitness for athletes and silently challenged every woman to be better than she ever believed she could be. Women everywhere took up the cross and rose to the challenge. Women's tennis attained a level higher than ever before, and Martina was the mentor and example. She also was mine. She also was my sons'. We were all better for having known her—not because of her fame or her money, but because of her example of courage, determination, and discipline on and off the court.

Most people know of her attributes on the court, but off the court, she was equally talented. She loved playing football for instance. She could compete with Roger Staubach when it came to quarterbacking. One of her favorite things was to throw passes with Eddie and Bales, Joe Breedlove, her personal trainer, and Randy Crawford, her coach for a year, on the beach whenever they were near one. The sand made a great surface for running and doing flying, outstretched leaps for the football when the passer threw the perfect ball. She loved reaching way out, making the spectacular catch, and rolling into the soft sand. It was also great exercise for her aerobically and physically. All the games that she played with the boys helped keep her fit. It was even a way of changing the routine of real workouts. She was the kind of girl every boy wished lived next door.

They say, however, that love is blind. Not all was perfect,

although in my mind it was. Just as with Ed, I did not see my faults, nor did I see hers. I stepped into a homosexual relationship and functioned just as I had in my heterosexual one. I was so busy "taking care of," I had little time to notice that there must be things about myself I needed to change—things that would eventually lead to the destruction of this "forever" relationship. Little did I know that Martina, too, needed to grow. On the tennis court she was brave and bold and seemingly in control. Off the court she wanted no responsibilities whatsoever. She needed a partner to assume that role. I was a perfect choice. Taking responsibility, taking control, is what I had done since I was a child. I could do it. Martina would have nothing to worry about except how many records she could break. Speaking of which, I believe with all my heart, that *nine* is enough—Wimbledons that is. There was no greater moment in the history of tennis, in my opinion, than on that Saturday on center court at Wimbledon when Martina won her ninth singles title to set the record that placed her above all others in that auspicious arena. She was, at that moment, I think, all she had ever wanted to be. She was Martina, the queen of Wimbledon's center court. She said in an interview later that she could die and go to heaven happy and satisfied, knowing that she had achieved all she had ever hoped for. She had all the money and luxuries that she ever needed, and she had the relationship she wanted for all her life. She could want no more. That was then.

At that most historic moment, another historic moment took place. Martina climbed through the stands and up into the "players' box" on center court and hugged her coaches Craig Kardon and Billie Jean King. She then turned to me, and we embraced for a long and tender moment that would be captured on the television sets of most of the world. The heterosexual world and homosexual community came together for one brief moment to witness with pride the victory of a woman who was often misunderstood and more often prejudged because of her sexual preference, but who was proud of both her victory and her sexuality. Neither of us had anything to hide. "Martina embraced her longtime companion, Judy Nelson," were the words of Chris Evert on NBC television. Chris would later tell me laughingly that she didn't know what she was going to say if the hug had lasted any longer! At that moment we were accepted by all the world. The feeling would be shortlived. I would not be at Wimbledon the following year to see Martina attempt to win her tenth singles victory. I would be in Texas still devastated that our relationship was over. I would also be trying to hold up under the fire of Martina and the media as they harshly judged that I had wrongly filed a lawsuit against her, demanding that she uphold a partnership agreement she had made with me some five years prior. My timing was also in question because the lawsuit was filed just before Martina left for England in preparation for Wimbledon. Lawyers do not care if somebody somewhere is playing a tennis tournament. They follow the law and are paid to do their job. Their job has no calendar. I, for once, had no control over the timing.

I had spoken with Martina before she left for Wimbledon in late May, asking if she would make a loan to me. I would repay it when all was settled between us. I had not had access to any money or credit cards, and my car and health insurance had been canceled, ever since the day after Martina departed. I told her I needed only enough money to pay my bills until September after she played at the U.S. Open, at which time I felt she would have a moment to sit down and work out some sort of settlement with me. At first she agreed, but the next day she called to say that after she had spoken with her attorneys, she could not loan me any money.

I had no means of support. I was getting deeper in debt each month. I could not hold out any longer. I called my attorney and childhood friend, Jerry Loftin, and told him of the new crisis. He said that he did not think I had any choice but to file the suit at that time. I gave him my consent. The deed was done. It was like putting a noose around my neck. Everyone would have a shot at me. Shoot they did.

But I would be a fool to reflect solely upon the end of our relationship. I will shed more light on that later. For now I want to recall the moments of joy, of love, of passion, and of glory. If there were a book of lesbian fairy tales, ours would be in it. Only the ending would need to be changed.

The fairy tale began in March of 1984. Martina and I had lunch together after her tennis practice in preparation for a tournament to be held in Dallas. She injured her leg at that practice. That was fate, I suppose, for it was because of that injury that she had to withdraw from the tournament, giving us unusual leisure time to develop and explore our newfound admiration for and attraction to one another. The next six weeks would present me with feelings and choices and with excitement and fears that I had never before even imagined. The question has been posed many times: Would I have fallen in love with a *woman* had it not been the great and rich and famous Martina? For many years I was not able to answer that question—how could I? I knew only that I loved her and it didn't matter who she was. It is, however, a question that I want to try to address. Yes, now I believe that it had to be Martina. She was a bigger-than-life, confident, and powerful woman. Since I didn't have any idea that it was a woman that could and would fulfill my empty love life, it is no wonder that it took someone as self-assured as Martina to approach me. I didn't know any lesbians in Fort Worth. I'm sure there were many, but none of them had any reason at all to seek me out. I wasn't out looking for women and they weren't out looking for me. For all practical purposes, to the community of Fort Worth, I was, as they so many times said in trashy newspaper articles, "the blond, Texan beauty queen, heterosexual, mother of two." No one, *no one* had any reason to think or believe that I would be happier with a woman. I was in the eyes of the world a

dyed-in-the-wool heterosexual. If I didn't even know any lesbians, how the hell was I ever going to know if I felt anything
romantically for another woman? Martina made the move; she
called and set the date. I responded. I was delighted and proud
that she had singled me out. There was not a way in the world
that I was not going to accept that invitation. The fact that she
might or might not be a lesbian just didn't even enter my mind.
I'll tell you, though, I'm glad she was, and I'm even happier
that she found me attractive and desirable. I surely did not
know what to do with the attention, but I was bound and
determined to find out. Find out I did. If I was truly going
crazy at this point in my life, I was at least going to die happier than I had ever been.

The fact that Martina would want to support me and my
sons did not seem unusual to me either. Remember that I was
brought up to think that my spouse was *supposed* to take care
of me, especially financially, and in return I would take care of
everything else. It is very generational and very Southern to
think in those terms. Even though I was prepared to do my
part with the finances if necessary, I still thought in those
terms. With Martina it would not be necessary. She made that
clear. She said that she had enough money for all of us, and
that what she needed and wanted was for me to be physically
with her all of the time. I was. Sometimes I would feel guilty
that I had to be gone from home so much or that I didn't gen-
erate any income. Except for the money I got each month from
my divorce settlement, Martina paid for everything. But even
that check went directly to our financial advisers, for we were
never in one place long enough to get mail, especially a check
that would need depositing. Sometimes I would suggest to her
that I stay at home in Fort Worth more often and get a job, or
create one, because I felt guilty. I had worked during most of
my marriage in some capacity or another and knew that I could
again if needed. She said no, she made enough. In the end
those words would come back to haunt me when she and

almost everyone else in the lesbian community would chastise me for wanting her to be responsible to me, Eddie, and Bales financially, because she had *already* given my family and me such an abundant life.

I did try to help secure endorsements for her. I continually came up with new ideas and would pursue them by making the appropriate contacts. I then turned them over to her manager (as I was always told I should do) to do the "real" negotiations. At one point, when she had no clothing contract, I designed her clothes and my mother sewed them into wonderful tennis outfits. She played in them at the U.S. Open in 1989, and they were such a hit that we had many people interested in producing the entire line. I was given the go-ahead to pursue this endeavor if I could pull it off. I did. Herman Geist of New York bought the right to manufacture the tennis clothing. A gala event at the Plaza Hotel kicked off the new venture. I had created something. I was adding to our domain. I was proud. The partnership and clothing line would be dissolved after Martina left. She wanted no attachment to me. She certainly didn't want me to make any more money "off her name," as she so openly stated. We all lost, I think.

Life on the road, jetting from one city to another, staying in one hotel after another, having room service or going out to dinner, seems so glamorous, but isn't. It is hard. I admire athletes all the more for being able to withstand such rigorous schedules and still maintain their sanity. Often you wake up confused as to where you are and even what day it is. We tried to devise ways to make each hotel or apartment seem familiar. We would take our own pillows, comforter, and feather bed mattress with us to make each new bed feel the same. We took our five dogs and two cats with us every place that we could. On the weekends, my sons and often my parents and sometimes hers would join us for the tournament. She was always in the final so one could count on a weekend of matches. There were no days off for the champion. She always played a final on Sunday and the next tournament would begin in another city or state or country on Monday. We would travel on that day as tournaments gave her a playing schedule to fit her victorious needs.

Her diet became more streamlined over the years. Her fitness was her calling card. No one was better. No one was more fit. Before arriving in a new town, we would find out where its health-food stores were located. We would often travel with special foods (without preservatives) that we knew would be hard to find. In hotels we asked for a small kitchen whenever possible so that I (or my mother or sometimes her mother) could cook certain dishes for her, such as pastas and vegetables, especially right before her practices and matches. If there was no in-room kitchen, we met with the hotel chefs and gave specific instructions as to how to prepare her food— without oils or any kind of fat. We would give them the groceries that we had bought or brought. If food was not prepared perfectly, it was immediately sent back to the kitchen. Whenever possible, we rented an apartment or small house for the week or weeks of the tournament, and then the question of proper and exact food preparation was solved. I did it.

My father, when he was along, was the best grocery shopper anyone had ever seen. He had the grocery list pretty much memorized. Often he made friends with the policemen who were stationed nearby to guard Martina's privacy, and they would escort him to do his errands each morning at the grandslam events because the traffic, especially at Wimbledon, was impossible. My mother would wash, clean, and iron for us at these events. She worked tirelessly and endlessly, often missing Martina's matches to get everything done. It was like taking your home on the road. It worked. It may have seemed odd or even extreme to outsiders, but it worked. We were a family. We all worked hard, except for the kids, and they just played hard. They were just kids. We all loved her. We were all proud of her. We were all there for her, always. She won and she won and she won. She was a happy camper. We gave her all that we could—most of that was love and lots of hard work. She gave us back the same. It was a different kind of family. We had to create our own pattern, our own structure, yet it worked. She was the champion and the breadwinner, but we all did our parts to make the surroundings happy, healthy, and emotionally supportive.

Romantically speaking, there just was no better couple than the two of us. We never showed affection in public, except perhaps with the eyes. But we loved to sneak away to the movies and hold hands in the darkness of the theater. Kissing was reserved for the bedroom. I remember that *Tennis Magazine* ran a write-in contest where readers could vote for their favorite "tennis couple." Our names were listed among all the heterosexual couples such as John McEnroe and Tatum, Jimmy Connors and Patty, and Chris Evert and Andy (or it may have been John Lloyd at that time). We won. Now that was a giant step! To some it may have been just a silly little thing, but to me it meant the world. We were accepted. We were a couple and nobody cared about which sex!

Life among the tennis elite was interesting, to say the least. The best part was realizing that they were just regular folks. Girls had cramps and guys had headaches. On the other hand, part of their world would never seem quite normal. Often at a very young age they are idolized and put on pedestals and seduced by enough contracts and endorsements and money to support them and their families and even friends for a lifetime with little attention given to their emotional needs and growth. I think something is very lopsided about a society that creates and supports that kind of scenario. But it's there, the theme is forever present, and I cannot complain much because I, too, enjoyed the benefits of the society that supported and encouraged the lifestyle of the rich and famous. After our breakup, Martina was once quoted as saying that "Judy would rather go to a party at Don Johnson's house than have dinner with my parents." That may have been true, but not for the reason implied—for I would rather have dinner with *my* parents than go to Don Johnson's. It's an in-law thing. I know everyone knows what I mean. A real insight into my character might have been to say that I would rather ride a horse than drive a Mercedes. No matter what, nor how varied my experiences, I still consider myself a down-home girl. I love the land. I love animals. Actually I think that is one of the best things that Martina and I had in common. And as for my in-laws, well, I loved them because they were her parents, but there was definitely a language barrier. My Czech was nonexistent, and their English was only good when it needed to be. They were never delighted that Martina chose to live with women. But she supported and housed them, so they couldn't knock it too much.

The tennis tour schedule was grueling. Yet, it was a way of life for most of the players. Some had played professionally since they were fourteen. They didn't know any other way to live. It was normal to them. It's how they earned a living, and for the most part they loved what they did, especially when they were victors. Martina was the best of them all, at least during the years that we were together. One can speculate that she would have been that successful without me and without the support of her new family, but I like to think that she was in part as successful as she was because she was happy and stable, and emotionally supported and fulfilled. It was hard in those days, and even in these, to be a lesbian and have family support. She had support; she even had a family with two sons. They were mine by blood. They were hers by choice.

Speaking of sons and young players, I remember the first time I ever saw Gabriella Sabatini. She was fourteen. Even then she was a talented player and sensational looking. One knew that she was going to grow up to be a beautiful woman. She has not disappointed anyone. My son Eddie was thirteen at that time. He thought she was really something. When he became fifteen, he insisted that we invite Gabby to have dinner with all our family at a favorite restaurant called Moonrakers, located somewhere between Eastbourne and Wimbledon. We did and he was the envy of every teenage boy back in Fort Worth at Country Day School. When he was eighteen and at the tennis tournament in Los Angeles, he actually asked her out on two dates. He was hot stuff! Gabby is as nice as she is beautiful. I was happy that he had such good taste. Ted Tinling, the "godfather" of women's tennis, used to say in a most complimentary way that "Gabby had the face of an angel and walked like John Wayne." And come to think of it, that's right on the money. Ted Tinling, in my book, was one very special human being. He always accepted my relationship with Martina with no questions asked. I loved him especially for that. Women's tennis lost something unique and dear when he died in 1988.

When I recall things that surrounded Martina and Gabriella, I cannot omit one of my fondest and funniest stories. Martina and Gabby were to play in a final against each other for the first time, at Hilton Head, South Carolina. The media had hyped it to be the event of the year. Gabby was the beautiful, young upstart who could play on clay as well if not better than anyone since Chris Evert. Chris had recently retired and was going to be a commentator on the match for NBC. Martina was the legend, but she hated to play on clay as it was the surface least suited to her serve-and-volley style. It also tested her patience. She had very little on the court, and that is why she played the way she did. She just wanted to get the point over as quickly as possible.

On the evening before the final on Sunday, Martina was soaking her tired body in the bathtub in the condo provided for us. I was in the bedroom when I heard a loud scream and then deep, deep sobbing. I rushed into the bathroom to find that Martina had bitten down on a raw carrot and knocked out most of her front tooth. She had beautiful teeth due mainly to the genius of a wonderful dentist and friend in New York, Dr. Michael Iott. She held the tooth in one hand as giant tears rolled down her face, and she capped her other hand over her mouth as she muffled the words, "I can't play tomorrow. I can't go on national TV with everyone watching me play the gorgeous Gabriella with my front tooth missing."

I tried to comfort her, then dashed for the phone to call Dr. Iott and prayed that he would be at home. Unbelievably he was. He answered right away. I told him the story. He told me, as I was still in midsentence, to find a way to get him from Atlanta to Hilton Head, and he would go straight to the airport to catch the first flight he could get to Atlanta. It was already about 8:30 P.M. on Saturday night. He hung up. Click, he was gone. Next I called Atlanta, as he had suggested, asking about connecting flights into Hilton Head that night. There were none. Oh, no. I called La Guardia Airport in New York, trying to find a flight that Michael may have caught. After explaining the incredible story several times (for officials were not supposed to give out passenger information on the phone), I finally found that he had indeed gotten aboard a Delta flight. I got the arrival time. I called the private airlines in Atlanta. They had no pilots to fly small aircraft that evening as there had been an air show that day and every private plane and pilot had flown all the hours for that day that the FAA would allow. I said there must be someone. Finally, one man was thought of who had not participated. He was called and awakened. He picked up Michael in Atlanta and flew him directly to Hilton Head. Michael arrived at our condo at 2:30 A.M. on Sunday morning by cab. I called a local dentist at home, who said that he would be happy to open his office on Sunday morning and let Michael go in and repair Martina's broken tooth. He did. She played. She won. It was just another Sunday on the road, another feather in her cap. She grinned from ear to ear.

At the grand-slam tournaments, where both the men and women played, there was another kid I remember, a tall, lanky, redheaded, freckled-faced young boy. Boris Becker was fifteen when I first met him. He had a big smile as well and a heart as huge as he was. The word had come to our camp that all he wanted to do was to hit with Martina. He loved the way she served and volleyed, and his admiration for her fitness and style on the court was immense. His coach asked if he could warm up with Martina on the grass practice courts in Melbourne before the Australian Open that year. He was just a boy. I loved watching him. He would run and tumble and fall on his knees and elbows just to make a shot in practice. He loved the game, one could tell. He loved Martina—one could tell that, too. No one was more proud of Boris when he won his first Wimbledon than Martina. She, of course, had won that year, too. It was Martina's sixth Wimbledon singles victory. The year was 1985.

Some interesting characters were on the tour. Some were not players; some were coaches, some just mentors. One of the ones I liked the most was Pancho Segura. When I met him, he was still coaching Andre Agassi. He was just who he was and I liked that. He was a champion player in his day, right beside greats like Pancho Gonzales. Sometimes he would sit beside me during some of Martina's matches, as he loved, like most, to watch her aggressive style. I'll never forget one year at the U.S. Open when he was sitting with me in the players' box watching one of Martina's early-round matches. It began to rain and the match was delayed until it stopped and the court could be dried. He turned to me and casually said, "You know, Judy, there are only two things you can do when it rains, and I don't like to read!" I never laughed so hard in my life and I've never forgotten what he said. I do like to read, but I'll have to agree with Pancho, there *is* one thing better!

The years with Martina were among the happiest years of my life. Like any couple, we had our misunderstandings and the usual ups and downs, but we were basically a happy couple. We gave to each other. We supported each other—all in ways much more important than financial ones.

We were a good team on and off the court. I remember the time when Martina and I, with no real knowledge, repaired Katharine Hepburn's TV set so that she could watch Martina's U.S. Open match one year. We had dropped by her home to leave her some chocolates, as we often did when in New York, and to invite her to sit in the players' box during Martina's final at the Open. She, understandably, could not attend, but she said that she always watched Martina on TV. That day, however, she had lost the reception on her set. Martina and I got down on hands and knees and began to tinker with it, moving and changing wires and controls until miraculously the most beautiful color picture appeared on the screen. We jumped for joy but didn't have any idea what we had done to get the picture. Kate was delighted, and Martina and I had a new profession.

We loved calling and going by to see Katharine when we had a free moment while in New York. We could sit and listen to her tell stories all day long. We would sit in a little parlor, enjoying a cup of tea, while listening in awe to this marvelous woman speak.

I recall the first time Martina and Kate ever spoke. It was on the telephone, a call initiated by Martina with my gentle encouragement. It had long been known that Katharine was Martina's hero and idol, and Katharine was known to hold Martina in some reverence. Kate loved tennis. She had been known to say that when she died, she would like to come back as a professional tennis player. Martina had sent some roses for Kate's birthday, having never even met her. Word got back to us that she would actually love to meet Martina. We secured Miss Hepburn's phone number, and Martina finally dialed it. Martina was prepared for anyone to answer the phone except Katharine herself. In that unmistakable voice, she answered. I watched Martina's face grow pale. Her mouth wanted to form words, but no sound came out. Then, after what seemed like minutes, the words began to flow erratically and nervously at first, but then with more comfort and confidence. I heard Martina say, "Miss Hepburn, this is Martina." And the voice I heard by leaning over close to the earpiece replied, "Well, it's about time." That was their introduction. They arranged to get together for tea at some near date, and I was invited as well.

I still send and receive notes from Kate. I have a special one that she sent me after she heard about our breakup. It is so clear and direct. I appreciate it even more now because I understand her words better. It is something I will always treasure. When I'm in New York, I still drop by and leave chocolates from time to time. Katharine is a woman for all seasons.

I acknowledge that in many ways Martina, like Hepburn, is still one of my heroines. Once after Margaret Court had publicly repudiated Martina's accomplishments because of her lifestyle, stating that she should never be considered a role model for the youth of today, a Martina fan had some buttons made up that read, "Martina is my role model." I proudly wore one along with hundreds of other people.

Martina was wonderfully childlike off the court. She was playful, witty, and funny. Actually she could probably have been a stand-up comedian if she had wanted. She could tell a joke with the best of them. Her punch-line timing was impeccable. What was even more impressive was her ability to remember jokes. She never forgot one once she heard it. I liked that.

Martina also loved mind games. She was constantly asking Mike Estep, her coach for some years, to teach her how to play bridge. They would have practice games on the airplane, getting Mike's wife, Barbara, to be a third, and sometimes I would help out and be the fourth.

Martina was excellent at anything that had to do with numbers. She has long been known in the tennis community for being able to remember scores and even points for all the matches she had ever played. I never saw her fail to come up with the right answers when questioned. This unique recall ability was also the reason she was so good at card games or backgammon and such.

Many agree that at tennis she may be the best of all time, but few people realize that she is such an exceptional athlete that she could probably have been a professional (and probably the best) in any sport she chose. From firsthand experience I can vouch for her driving expertise. Most people know that Martina loves fast cars and motorcycles. I sat beside her in a Porsche 959, an experimental model of which only about a hundred were made, when she drove it 204 miles per hour down the autobahn in Germany. We were going so fast that I couldn't see anything, so I just read a book that I had brought along. When I had the sensation that the car had actually lifted off the ground, I looked up and calmly asked, "How fast are we going?" She replied, "About two hundred and four." I said, "I think that's fast enough." There's only so much trust a person can stand! I was certain that at any moment she would push a button and wings would slide out of the doors and we would simply fly away sort of James Bond style.

I also loved her powerful persona on the tennis court. I watched every match and as many practices as time would allow. I never tired of seeing her play. For a long time after she left, I missed it. Watching her, encouraging her, and supporting her were so much a part of my life. I don't miss it anymore. Time and change heals us all, I suppose.

As I reflect upon those years with Martina, I remember the commitment we made to each other. We even exchanged vows in a church one Sunday morning in Brisbane, Australia, in 1985, then recommitted our lives to one another during a three-day honeymoon, when we finally had the time between tournaments, two years later in Venice.

I often wonder why I was given these choices. Why was this to be my path? Life in the heterosexual world is much easier. I automatically gave up all the perks and pleasures of a Southern belle the moment I became a lesbian. The risk of losing my children was also shockingly prevalent. What was I saying? I think I was at long last taking a step toward real equality and toward  assuming my own sense of power as a woman. No more silence. I was a woman without a man, voluntarily— choosing to do things for myself. But I got caught up in the very heterosexual role that I thought I was leaving. I remained the caretaker. The pattern by which the family functioned was almost the same. Martina was the breadwinner. I was the wife, mother, caretaker, and all-around do-everything-elser. I see it now. I didn't see it then. I tell you, though, I fell in love with a woman as simply and honestly and as easily as I had fallen in love with my husband seventeen years earlier—as odd as that may seem to a predominantly heterosexual world.

Not until after Martina left did I take the time to reflect on my decision. I had as many questions as the public had, it seemed. By being on the other side of the fence now, I think I can lay to rest several myths. Much to the disillusionment of the heterosexual community, lesbians do not go around trying to seduce "straight" women into what the radical right often refers to as their "sexually perverted" way of life. Martina did not seduce me or win me over. I was present. I was available. I just didn't recognize the signals. I think it is looking into a person's eyes and really seeing them that is the signal. It is the same signal given between a man and a woman. If it does not happen for both people, then the relationship won't bloom. It is the same for all couples. The look was in my eyes as well as Martina's at that first lunch in 1984. We both knew it. There was no premeditated seduction. It was real; it was thrilling; and I was scared to death. Was I a lesbian? The answer was yes, but I didn't know it. Was I falling in love with a woman? The answer was, most definitely, yes. Was I happy? Emphatically, yes.

I think most lesbians would simply like to fall in love with another lesbian. It takes a special kind of woman to be a lesbian, and in my opinion Southern heterosexual woman of my generation were not often allowed to develop such qualities. A lesbian is often self-assured and self-assertive, and usually unafraid of having to take care of herself, simply because she has to—she has no man to do it for her. Women of my generation were still taught to be dependent on their men. I hope that today that idea is changing. I think, however, that from time to time all women, straight or gay, have their doubts. It is still a man's world. We were taught this right out of the womb. It is a hard concept to escape because men still do not want to let us have power. The laws, the percentages of women in executive positions, the percentages of women holding public office, still reflect this same male-dominated world. Ours is still very much a patriarchal society.

One of the main problems I have with Martina's "love 'em and leave 'em" style, which is a quote from Rita Mae Brown, is that she then holds herself above the law because no laws govern lesbian and gay relationships. She advocates equal freedom for all, and yet she does not hold herself accountable when she leaves a relationship. Perhaps this is just one of the reasons that the heterosexual community does not value such relationships: because in the end, as demonstrated perfectly by Martina and all the others who raise her flag, we do not value our relationships either. The lesbian community condones the "no responsibility" philosophy once a relationship has ended, no matter how long it lasted, no matter how committed it was, no matter if children were involved. Martina, I think, must have felt betrayed because she says that I was not the person she thought I was, that in the end all I wanted was her money.

No, Martina, when it was really over, what I wanted was for you to be responsible for your promises and commitments. That did not mean half of everything that was made while we were together, even though that is what our agreement provided. It did mean that I did not think that you should have been allowed to walk away from a marriage, a wife, a caretaker, a partner, a mother, and two children (albeit adopted lesbian style) without at least recognizing that you had some responsibilities when that relationship failed and you no longer wanted it. It wasn't about betrayal, it was about denial. It was about your denial that you had any responsibility to me and Eddie and Bales whatsoever.

The heterosexual community places some value on the support role. Laws are made that protect heterosexuals when the breadwinner leaves the marriage.

I think that Martina's confusion is with the myth that good Southern women, when abandoned, will still be good. They will merely say, "Thank you so much for all that you've done for me while I was with you." I think the real Southern woman at that point often shows her strength and says, "Wait a minute, what I did and gave to this relationship, the endless support, is as valuable as all the money you gave to it." Perhaps the money is valuable, but the emotional support is invaluable.

In the end, Martina asked me, what I had ever done for her? I ask her now what I didn't have the courage to ask her then: "What didn't I do for you?" I shall quote a friend of mine regarding the issue, whose name will remain anonymous:

> Martina has stated that she was successful before her relationship with you. That may be true. But the real question is, how long would that success have continued? It is probably true to say that Martina was very self-assured on the court. But I for one did not witness the same self-confidence off the court, until she became involved with you. She was popular amongst the lesbian community, but there was a lavender ceiling so to speak. You helped her rise above that. I am hesitant to say that you softened her. Perhaps it is now appropriate to say that you were instrumental in helping the heterosexual community to understand who Martina was not. Meaning that she was not a lesbian predator who was out trying to convert young virgins. You brought a sense of normalcy to a very misunderstood lifestyle. This atmosphere allowed Martina wider access into arenas that had previously been off-limits. If Martina has a voice in politics or gay issues, it is in no small way a direct result of your efforts. You bodily knocked down doors and then held them open, allowing Martina to walk in first. Hey, I guess that makes you a butch.

Well, I guess it does. Which puts to rest another myth: that Martina was the "butch" and I was the "femme." I think there is a bit of butch and femme in each of us, and the one that steps forward in any given situation is the one needed.

If I had any of the salary that Martina says she gave me and if I had all those millions that people claim I received from Martina, then you would probably find me on some beach somewhere in the Caribbean sipping piña coladas and listening to reggae music. On second thought, I don't think Martina would have fallen in love with that person. Surely she must have seen something worth loving in me. I like to think so anyway.

I think that at times I was just an ornament to her, just like the ones that most Southern men I knew wanted. Was I just another trophy for Martina? Only Martina knows the answer. I rest my case.

But rest assured this does not mean that I ever loved Martina any less.

# 9

## IMG: The Power

I recognized the voice on the other end of the line immediately. It was Peter Johnson, from IMG (International Management Group), Martina's longtime manager. Peter and I had been friends for seven years. Today his voice was not friendly. It was all business.

International Management Group is one of the largest management companies that represent professional athletes in the world. It is known to most athletes as simply IMG. It was started years ago by a great guy named Mark McCormack. He began the company by first representing and securing endorsements and negotiating contracts for Arnold Palmer. They were buddies. The company now has offices and representatives all over the world. They are big, multifaceted, and very, very powerful. They provide athletes who sign exclusive contracts with them with personal managers. This was Peter Johnson's role in Martina's life and in mine while I was with her. We worked closely together. He always listened to my ideas and would run his ideas by me. He would usually contact me rather than Martina because he was careful not to disturb her during a tournament. He would rely on my timing for delicate or important issues. I appreciated his confidence in me.

The first time I ever talked to Peter Johnson face-to-face was in 1984, and he took me aside in a little office at a tournament somewhere and tried his best to explain the situation I was getting myself into—life on the professional tennis circuit. "It is not as glamorous as it is cracked up to be, and the media can be cruel and damaging, especially to Martina," he said. "Be careful, they [the media] can hurt you, too." He knew that they already had and that they were hounding my family and my sons as well. He told me that I would need to take care of everything for Martina. He said that she was the number one player in the world, but that she plays best only when she is focused on playing tennis, nothing else. He said that it was my job to see to it that she was happy and not disturbed by anyone or anything. I told him that I understood and that I felt I could do the job. He said, "Be careful, it's a tough world out there." I said, "I know."

The last time I ever talked to Peter Johnson, some seven years later in 1991, was not face-to-face. His words were unequivocal: "Judy, you don't want to file a lawsuit against Martina. You better take anything she offers you and go home. We are too big and too powerful, and we will ruin you financially and emotionally. Let it alone. That's my advice." He was dead serious. For perhaps the first time in my life I knew what real fear was. I was all alone in our house in Aspen. No family was around me for support. People who I had thought were friends were already beginning to abandon me right and left. It was much like in the beginning of my relationship with Martina. Then, as now, I would begin to know who my real friends were, and Peter Johnson was not one of them. As a matter of fact, financial advisers at IMG would barely return my phone calls, and I was given little or no information about my financial situation ever again. They had been my advisers as much as Martina's because we did everything jointly—or so I was led to believe. They used me. They used my talents. They used my influence with Martina. They led me to believe that they were doing things for my benefit as well. They were not. It was *all* about Martina. I was naive.

When they first told me that they were going to set up a salary for me as Martina's manager, I said, "Fine." I asked no questions. I never even asked to see a paycheck. I never saw one either. I did not have a separate checking account. All the things we did, we did jointly, or so I thought. I was told by our financial adviser that I was to go on the books as an employee of Martina Enterprises. I was told at one of our brief financial meetings (which Martina hated) that my first salary was to be $35,000 a year. A couple of years later they told me that it would be raised to $50,000 a year. I said, "Fine." I had never asked for a salary anyway. I never saw a paycheck. Just a few months before Martina left me they said they needed to increase my salary to $90,000 a year. I said, "Fine." I never asked why. I still never saw a paycheck. Now how dumb is all of that?

When she left and even today in interviews, Martina leaves the media and the public with the false impression that I received all that money ($90,000 a year) for *all* those years. People think I must have it all saved up in some bank account somewhere. It is no wonder to me that by that statement alone people question why I needed to file a suit against Martina to try to get *more* money. The fact is that I didn't have that money. Never did. Never saw it. I doubt that it would have covered my airfare and hotel bills for one year had I actually received it. On paper, and on our financial statements, it must have looked good. But I never once saw a paycheck made out to me or, needless to say, endorsed by Judy Nelson. I hope that is another myth put to rest.

It was amazing to me that all during our relationship our home, or homes, were referred to by Martina and our friends, and everyone at IMG, as *our* home. After Martina left, it was referred to by Martina, Peter Johnson, our financial advisers, and our friends as *Martina's* home. It was as though I had never lived there, never cooked there, never entertained there, never slept there, never had my toothbrush there, never hung my kids' pictures on the walls there. It was truly as if it had been *her* house, and my sons and I had merely been visitors in it for seven years.

I should have been at least a little curious all those years when at our financial meetings Martina would sometimes suggest that the house or ranch property be in both our names, and always the IMG advisers would be quick to reply, "No, that's not a good idea for tax reasons, you know." I never questioned that either. I just accepted whatever was put before me. I did think it a little odd, because I was accustomed to a heterosexual marriage where houses and cars are, more often than not, put in both names, unless there is a prenuptial agreement to do otherwise. I was given every indication that IMG was looking after my needs and financial security as well as Martina's, but obviously they were not. I was dispensable. Martina was not.

They did do one good thing for me, and I am most grateful. I'm certain they would have found a way to keep that, too, had it not been put in my name. They created an IRA account for me, and I learned many months after Martina left that it had about $90,000 in it. They had to give it to me. I used the IRA to pay debts that had accrued during the months after Martina left, when I had no means of support. I incurred a 20 percent penalty for cashing it in early. Again I lost. Again I had no choice.

Get a job, you say? Right. This was the situation: I've just lost the love of my life. I am devastated. I have devoted my life to her and her endeavors for the past seven years. I have two sons both going to college. I'm living in a house and a town that I cannot afford. I'm forty-five years old. I've worked all my life, but I always created my own jobs. Martina and the media are damaging my character in every interview. Martina was essentially my employer. Do you think she or IMG were going to give me a good recommendation? Do you think there was one employer who would have hired me with all the notoriety? Many people at that time knew who I was. If I left the house with all my things in it, would I ever see any of it again? My teacher's certificate was long outdated. At that point in my life, even *I* would not have hired me.

Yes, Peter Johnson was right. They would ruin me financially and emotionally. They were simply too powerful. Was there a conflict of interests on the part of IMG? I think so.

I felt like David and they were Goliath, only I didn't even have a slingshot and they were the ones throwing stones.

# 10

## The Media: Damaged Again

In the beginning, the media presented me as the woman who left her husband and two sons for the famous tennis star, Martina. I did not. But because of the power of the media, I am even today remembered that way. Probably no one single thing has hurt me more than that.

In the end, I was capsuled as a gold digger and the woman who betrayed Martina. These accusations were always neatly wrapped in tidy little quotes from Martina and unnamed sources, but never a quote from me.

I watched in shock in 1984 as reporters planted themselves outside my home in Fort Worth when they first heard rumors that I was Martina's next girlfriend. I was devastated when reporters followed my sons and their friends to the swimming pool and asked people questions about my personal life. They harassed my family and my estranged husband with phone calls requesting interviews. When interviews were denied, the tabloids often claimed exclusive interviews merely because they were able to get someone to answer the phone. I learned that the media, like IMG and Martina, had the power. With the written word they could change heaven into hell. In the beginning and in the end, they did exactly that to me. It's interesting, however, to note that in the middle years—years when Martina triumphed and the relationship flourished and seemed solid—the press became kinder to me. They met me personally. We spoke. We sometimes fraternized. We experienced joys and sometimes tears together as we witnessed Martina's victories and defeats. Journalists and I developed a camaraderie and a respect for each other. We were like a pair of old gloves that had become softer over time. Sometimes we shared a coffee or tea and a chat or a laugh. The media was always around the tennis circuit and its stars. I was there, too. Even the fact that we were a same-sex couple seemed less sensational, and we became accepted for the people we were rather than belittled for the label that had been given us. I, naively, never thought that those same reporters would turn on me at the breakup of our relationship, much as they had crucified me in the beginning before they came to know me. But power and money carry a lot of weight, and in the end I had neither.

Sadly, I understand that power. The power is in the written word, and that word is not good unless it is read. Who would the public rather have an interview from: Martina or Judy Nelson? Of course the fact that we were two women living together made it all the more sensational. The fact that I had lived most of my life as a heterosexual made it even more tantalizing.

In the end I did not expect Martina's ruthless attack on my character, nor did I expect the media to buy it hook, line, and sinker. I now realize that if it sells papers or makes a story, they do it. Simply put any personal feelings for the person aside and give the public a story they can devour.

Vultures like Harry Sisker, a freelance photographer, seemed at the time to come to the aid of the weak and frightened underdog. I was that. He marched in, took photos, and arranged for interviews, which I was promised I could approve before they would be printed. I never got to approve anything. I was hoping the interviews would reflect my views on our breakup and also offer insights into a misunderstood lifestyle. That was a joke. Harry Sisker lied and cheated and even took photos that I was unaware of and didn't authorize. He sold the photos to anyone who would pay his price, mostly tabloids in England and the *Enquirer* and *Globe* in the United States. He had writers interview me and write stories. I learned long after publication what the articles said and how my statements were taken completely out of context. Or in some cases sensationalized so that the words no longer resembled the intent. It was a lesson I shall never forget.

He did the same to Martina, only she was smart enough not to give him any arranged interviews. I heard at one point that she even took a swing at him. I wish I had. He still has personal pictures that I treasure, and even though I have placed many calls and faxes to him regarding them, I have never received them. I suppose I never will. I was the perfect target for a guy like Harry. I was weak and vulnerable and alone. I have been vulnerable since then. I have also been alone since then, but I hope I'm never that weak or naive again. He has no scruples. I do. I aim to keep mine intact.

There was also the TV broadcast of the videotape of the signing of my partnership agreement with Martina. Why was it on television at all? Why was everyone allowed to see what was to be so private? The reality is that, again, I could not change the law, and yet I was chastised in the press by Martina and others for "turning over a private tape" and creating a media circus. In reality the video was part of the agreement: it was our *witness* so to speak. Therefore, when the lawsuit was filed in 1991, the agreement and the video were turned over to the court. It was then in the "public domain," giving all the media and public access to it. I would have preferred that no one see it except the people who had to.

My attorneys and I also requested that no cameras be allowed in the courtroom during a hearing for my attorney, Jerry Loftin. This hearing would decide whether Jerry could represent me if our case ever went to court because of an alleged conflict of interest. That, and the allegation by Martina and her attorney, was filed in a suit against him. She even attempted to have him disbarred. The lawsuit against Jerry was not resolved until March 22, 1995, in an out-of-court settlement between Jerry's malpractice insurance company and Martina's attorneys. The case was forever closed. The media was no longer interested, and little was ever written about that settlement except bits and pieces in my hometown paper in Fort Worth. Jerry did nothing wrong. He suffered much. I am forever in his debt for his unwavering friendship, support, and counsel. The media made him out to be the guy in the black hat. Again the power was in the pen.

The media did not come crashing down on Ivana Trump during her divorce from Donald. Nor did it ever ridicule Tatum O'Neal during her divorce from John McEnroe. Even Tom Hayden, who received a settlement from Jane Fonda in a reversal of roles, never got blasted. So I ask myself, was all of this misguided and ill-placed attention put on our separation and settlement because we were two women? I think so. Why did the media come out in full opposition to one woman in the separation, or divorce, of two women when that woman was asking only to have the same protection and fairness under the law as any other married woman in the world would receive? I continue to question the media as to their interest in this matter. Why would they paint a white hat on Martina and allow her to walk away from a seven-year relationship without taking responsibility for it? We were a family. We had two sons. Should not the media have respected the vows and promises we made rather than making a mockery of them?

# 11

## The Attorneys: Who Reaped the Benefits?

The magnitude of the lawsuit I filed against Martina, maintaining the belief that she did indeed have some responsibility to me and to my sons when she left, sometimes overwhelmed me, and I would become despondent. At those times, Rita Mae Brown had me read the following verse from the Bible. It became a source of strength when I had none:

2 Timothy 4:7

*I have fought a good fight,*
*I have finished my course,*
*I have kept the faith.*

I did what I thought was just in the face of relentless opposition. I maintained that our relationship was as valuable as any heterosexual one and that the same rights and freedoms afforded other divorced couples should be afforded us. It was for some of those reasons that we established a partnership agreement in the first place. Since no laws provide guidelines for same-sex relationships, we decided to create an agreement to record our responsibilities to one another should we ever dissolve the commitment. We never thought that anything would ever destroy our relationship. We never thought we would ever have to open that envelope that held the document we had created or that we would ever have to view the video account of the signing of the contract. The thought of "never, ever" came from the magical world of Judy and Martina. The reality is, of course, that we never, ever really know. We can believe with all our hearts, and surely *we* did, but we can never be certain that anything is forever. That is not being cynical. It is being realistic. Being realistic is something I never wanted to be; I just wanted to be the romantic. I hope I am still a romantic, but in a more mature and wiser way.

With a lawsuit, in march the attorneys. All lawyers want their clients to win, because in so doing, *they* also win. Our case thankfully never went to court. Oddly, the public, for the most part, still does not realize that fact. I have come to realize that because of the way the famous Martina-crying-in-the-court-room scene was splashed across the television sets of many homes in America, the majority of the public thought, and still thinks, that it was a hearing for our case. It was not. It was a hearing to decide whether my attorney of choice, Jerry Loftin, would be allowed to represent me. Our side maintained there was no conflict of interest and hers contended there was. Martina and I settled our issues quietly one day in a room by ourselves behind closed doors, as our attorneys all waited anxiously in a room nearby.

After Martina left, it was difficult to have a one-on-one discussion with her. Things were tense and feelings were raw for both of us, I think. It is my nature to try to solve problems. I wanted to talk to her in person, but neither she nor her schedule would allow that. Martina told me that since the two of us couldn't see eye to eye on the agreement we had signed, all future dealings would have to go through her manager, Peter Johnson. She said that the issues were just too emotional for her. Peter became the middleman before the attorneys got involved. Martina's offer to me would barely have covered college tuition for Eddie and Bales. Likewise, the house she offered was a two-bedroom lake condo that she had verbally given to my parents. They had been living in it for two years at that point. Was I supposed to make them move out of a house she had always promised them? Or was I at age forty-five to move in with my parents? It was not an option. At that point Peter made his stoic threat with his IMG power and suggested that I take the offer and run. I refused.

The next thing I knew, Martina was back in Aspen for only a day or two to pick up some clothes from our house. She came in the side door as always. She pulled her car up close, and in only a matter of minutes she had packed duffels and loaded more of her skis and golf clubs. Her parting words were, "You better get a good attorney 'cause these guys that IMG had me meet with in Dallas yesterday are the best divorce attorneys in Texas. They told me the sorts of things they intended to do in this case and some of the questions they would ask you, and believe me, Judy, you don't want to mess with these guys. I wouldn't even answer some of their questions."

That proved to be no small statement. After the lawsuit was filed and depositions had to be taken, I sat at the head of a long conference table with only one other woman in the room. There were at least six men. I was drilled and grilled for eight hours. I was never asked about the content of our agreement. Aside from the basic who, what, where, and when questions, all of the how questions were of a sexual nature. I was embarrassed and humiliated. I did not see what those questions had to do with the lawsuit. I do not think any human being should be put through interrogation like that. Martina did not attend my deposition, although she had that right. I did, however, sit in on hers. My attorneys stuck to the issue at hand: the partnership agreement.

Martina's team of attorneys was headed up by a little man named Mike McCurly. He had slicked-back hair that curled up at the nape of his neck. He wore stacked-heeled cowboy boots and strutted into a room as if to take charge. He was good and he was expensive. He hired his own PR agent to be with him during Jerry Loftin's hearing. He arrived at the courthouse each day in a limousine. He held his own press conferences. Martina, too, arrived in limos for Jerry's hearings, although that was not unusual for her and often necessary. She, too, had her own PR agent from Los Angeles at her side. They would release preplanned press releases, and Martina would hold press conferences from time to time. Some things had not changed at all. The character attack on my parents and family a couple of days into the hearings made the front pages of the *Fort Worth Star Telegram*. My mother cried for days over Martina's comments. My dad was silent. Bales was hurt and Eddie was furious. Before court began on the morning of the newspaper character assault by Martina, she came over to my mother and hugged her and said that she was sorry. My mother, of course, told her it was all right. They told each other that they loved one another. That was the last time Martina ever spoke to my mother. That was in 1991.

My attorney, Jerry Loftin, was also tough. He had tried important and news-making cases. His demeanor was that of a good ole boy from Fort Worth. Jerry and his paralegal, BeAnn Sizemore, had been friends of mine before Martina and I ever got together. Jerry and I went all the way from junior high through college together. He and BeAnn became friendly with Martina, too. Jerry had helped Martina with a couple of traffic tickets, but they actually became friends when Jerry was helping me during my divorce from Ed. He had helped me six years before that when Ed had filed for a divorce. BeAnn had been a trusted and loyal friend to both of us through all the years of our relationship. In 1986 we called and asked BeAnn if she would help us find a copy of a standard partnership agreement that we could use rather than making it a big and public ordeal and pay huge attorneys' fees for having a more complicated agreement drawn up. IMG thought we should have one and we thought so, too, because our relationship was not protected by the laws that protect every other married couple in the world.

The stage was set. Both of us had a team of attorneys, all capable and ready to present their client's case. The first hurdle was, oddly, for Jerry and not me. Her attorneys claimed conflict of interest. This clever tactic diverted attention from the real issues and slowed down the process, which would of course be monetarily and emotionally difficult for me. As the days dragged into weeks and months, I became more and more in debt. I had to borrow money from my family and cash in my IRA to stay afloat while the judicial system slowly moved, at her expense and mine. The attorneys were making the money. After Mike McCurly charged Martina for a portion of the air-conditioning in his building when he had to work on weekends on the case, she fired him. A second set of attorneys who had already been assisting McCurly took over for Martina. They, I think, were less high maintenance.

Jerry, on the other hand, withdrew from the case in my best interest. The court never had to hand down a judgment on that issue.

Martina and I each retreated to our corners until the next round. When the next bell rang, I had a new team of attorneys. The famous "Racehorse" Richard Haynes from Houston had agreed to take my case. When we first met, he said, "Well, little lady, we're going to see if Texas is ready to move into the twenty-first century or not." I liked his style. I liked his principles. He was tough as nails. He looked you straight in the eye. He never minced words. He always told you how the "cow ate the cabbage." After he examined all the boxes of documents and papers dealing with the case, he decided that he would call in a friend, a giant among attorneys, Steve Sussman from Dallas. Sussman specialized in cases against large corporations. Racehorse and Sussman had decided that IMG needed to be included in the lawsuit for "conflict of interest." IMG had represented me as my financial adviser as well as Martina's. I was IMG's most direct contact to Martina. After they were named in the suit, things began to happen at a much speedier pace. Before I knew it, Martina had called and we were actually going to meet face-to-face, after over a year of foot-dragging, to try to settle our differences out of court. We did. The attorneys waited in a nearby conference room that day. We didn't even break for lunch; we just had something brought in and we kept on talking. Each of us knew we were getting close to a settlement, and neither of us wanted to go to court or prolong what had become a media heyday at our expense.

Speaking of expenses, I do not know what Martina ultimately had to pay in attorneys' fees. I shudder to think. My attorneys were on a retainer because I had no money to pay them by the hour. In the end they got 40 percent of the estimated value of the settlement. They promised to adjust their fees when I sold my house in Aspen based on what it *actually* sold for versus what we had previously estimated would be its value. They did not. I lost again but I had no fight left in me. I wasn't about to go up against my own attorneys. They wanted a percentage of the estimated value of the assets rather than the real value. I was powerless in my efforts to hold them to their promise.

But that was not the end of it all. I was harassed by Martina's attorneys for years after the settlement for one reason or another—over issues too tacky to even mention. For certain, they weren't going to let me walk away peacefully. They were not finished with their emotional draining, and the media wasn't done with its bloodletting. After all, it was all about two women, wasn't it? That always sells papers.

Amid all the darkness I was sent a bright light. Her name was Sandra Faulkner. She would become a staunch friend. She would ultimately write my story with me in the book *Love Match* which was about my seven years with Martina and my devastation at the end.

Sandra is a sociologist who owned a jury-behavior consulting company, out of Carmel, California. Because of her background in law and culture she was most interested in my case against Martina. She was also an avid tennis player and attended many Virginia Slims and grand-slam events. Being a student of the game, she often had an uncanny grasp of it and of the sacrifices it takes to be a champion. For all these reasons I felt that Sandra was the perfect person to tell my story. Besides all those attributes, she was and is a most compassionate and trustworthy human being. Those two characteristics were the most important to me. Thus we spent much time together talking, crying, and sometimes even laughing. She helped me through some difficult times. For that, I am eternally grateful.

My family was also an unflagging source of support during those stressful months of the court case. That alone amazes me when I reflect on it, for their pain was also great, their loss was also deep, and the character assaults that were directed at them were damaging. Somehow they were all able to hold their heads high and walk proudly among the community that chastised me. They bore my burden and never complained. They attended to my needs and nurtured me. They were my strength and my direction.

Even after Martina and I had agreed on a settlement, the saga was not finished. Martina's attorneys still maintained that Jerry Loftin was wrong to initially represent me; they, therefore, pursued the lawsuit against him. They also wrote letters to the Texas Bar Association in an attempt to have him disbarred. It would certainly make their case against him look good if the bar would at least reprimand him. He was never disbarred. At the disbarment hearing some months after our settlement was signed, I saw Martina for the last time. That was in 1992. I have not seen Martina since. She is an image on TV for me much as she is to the rest of the world. I find that strange and sometimes unsettling. We didn't even speak that day. I sat at a table with BeAnn

Sizemore, and Martina was in another room making phone calls most of the time. After she testified against Jerry, she asked for permission to leave early because she had a plane to catch. Whisk—she was off. Her lifestyle had not changed much as far as I could see. My deep and tender feelings for her had been numbed a bit by all the false accusations, and I watched her leave the dark room filled with panels of attorneys sitting in folding chairs behind temporary tables. It was a lifeless ending to a vibrant love affair. She was gone from my life forever. I've talked to her a couple of times on the phone since then. Her voice was foreign and cold. I must have hurt her terribly. I challenged her to the core. Off the tennis court no one else ever had.

In 1995, some four years later, Jerry's professional slate was wiped clean. The dangling and irritating lawsuit by which Martina and her legal teams were attempting to recoup what she had given me and what she had spent in attorneys' fees had finally been set on the court's docket. The judge ordered both teams of attorneys to mediation just days before the case was to be heard. An out-of-court settlement was reached. I still think Jerry wanted to fight the case and exonerate himself of any wrongdoing, but I think his malpractice insurance company must just have wanted the whole thing over.

I never speak to Racehorse. He did his job. His reputation as a major figure among attorneys probably helped speed up the turtlelike process. Perhaps that's how he got his nickname. Steve Sussman faded out as quickly as he had faded in. At any rate, I'm grateful to them both. But I learned another lesson: you get more for your money if you pay attorneys by the hour. If you pay just a retainer, I know who reaps the benefits.

BeAnn Sizemore went back to school to get her law degree to become an attorney. I like that. Women can do it for themselves.

Enough trying to set the records straight and complaining about injustices. You either grow from your mistakes and you move forward or you wallow in them and remain stagnant.

# 12

# Where Did All My Friends Go? Again?

I have heard it said more than once that if you can count your true friends on more than one hand then you are lucky. I don't think it is luck. I think it is a gift. Thus, I have been blessed. Although many people in my life professed to be my friends, when the path became rocky, they fell by the wayside. My true friends have stayed by my side and proven to be my armor and my stability, never making judgments about my extraordinary choices.

It has been my experience that the kids whom I grew up with seem to be less judgmental of my very public choices than the friends whom I met in college and early marriage. Perhaps that has something to do with the innocence of youth. I think the older I got the more guarded I became of who I was or was not and of my successes or failures. The energy spent in relationships in my youth was with my peers; in adulthood that energy was spent primarily with my family—my husband and sons. In young adulthood time spent with girlfriends was limited. Remember, having boys as friends was always hard because of the sexual undercurrent that after some time always showed itself. Not until my children were in middle school was I able to spend any meaningful time with my girlfriends as I had in my adolescence. Even at that, only a few special friends from my years with Ed have remained unapprehensive about maintaining a bond with me.

Almost everyone with whom I had spent my extracurricular time abandoned me after they realized that I had chosen to live with Martina. The reasons were as far-fetched as that their children would be exposed to a lifestyle that was unnatural. They were afraid their children might begin to imagine that such a lifestyle could be a choice for them, especially since paradoxically we appeared normal and happy and successful. They were willing to admit that other same-sex relationships might appear happy, but they were by no means normal, and Martina's success was an exception to the rule. I could not believe their vision was so narrow. I often wonder when hetero-sexuals make such proclamations, do they not remember the great poets and writers, artists and entertainers, who have been homosexual? Martina is but one of many who have been famous and successful.

When I think of the friends I had—the women I carpooled with, had lunch with, played tennis with—I wonder how my choice of partner could have threatened them so much that they felt they could no longer be friends with me. It was as though all of a sudden we had nothing in common. It does lead me to examine upon what basis I had built my friendships. Per-haps it is different now. I certainly am more willing to allow people to see more of who I really am rather than just that part of me I think they want to see or that they would like.

After Martina came into my life, I made other new friends. There were the women who worked for the Women's Tennis Association, the WTA, other tennis players and their families, and people who worked for various tournaments. Also, many friends of Martina's became mine. Of all those people, the ones who stood beside me after she left can be counted on my fingers.

The same fans of Martina's who cheered me, now jeered me. Their scorn was quick and incisive. I had never been the enemy of so many women in my life. I realize that these people were probably not ever really my friends, that through me they were simply getting closer to Martina. The rejection I felt was still devastating.

I remember being *un*invited to a baby shower for Chris Evert. Claire Evert, Chris's sister, was the tennis pro at the Aspen Club at that time. After Martina left, I started taking lessons from Claire. I had not played tennis seriously in eight years. Claire was an excellent teacher, and a friendship developed because of so many mutual experiences and acquaintances. Claire called up and asked me to a baby shower for Chris in Aspen. I was delighted that I was invited. Chris and I had been good friends for a lot of years. We used to talk a lot about having and raising kids. I was the only one around the women's tennis circuit who had children. Then, only two days before the party, I was uninvited. One of the other ladies giving the luncheon called and asked me not to come. Martina's schedule had changed and she was going to be in Aspen at the time of the shower. Chris herself called me later to say that she was sorry but that Martina would not attend if I was present. Chris said that she had not gotten to spend much time with Martina since her retirement and really wanted to see her. I said that I understood and then cried for days.

Although I lost many of the friends that I had known while I was with Martina, a handful stood by me in the face of pressure from Martina and others to disassociate themselves from me. The kind of courage it took for those people to remain my friends meant more to me than those people probably know. Neither did they abandon Martina. They just simply did not see why they had to choose one or the other of us. I did not either.

Several other important relationships developed during that year and a half that I stayed in Aspen. Mindy Nagel was one. Mindy was the pro at the Grand Champions Tennis Club. She, Claire Evert, and I played a lot of tennis together. The first time I ever met Mindy, she was on the other side of the net from me during a match at the club's tennis tournament. She hit a little dink-type volley at me that went right between my legs. I looked like a fool. I looked up at her and smilingly and quietly said, "You bitch." It was in jest of course, but we still laugh about those being the first words ever exchanged between us. I told her a few minutes later on the changeover that *bitch* was a term of endearment. When my sons were young and trying out new phrases to shock me, *bitch* was one of the choice words. I hated it and forbade them ever to use it, so of course they used it all the more. I then decided to join them rather than fight them. I began to use the word in a happy and lighter context. Whatever the psychology, it worked. All of us laugh about it even today. Mindy laughed, too. I love her. We've been friends ever since. She will always be a special person in my life.

Mindy and Claire Evert gave me another very, very special friend, Nellie. Nellie is my beautiful golden retriever. She is named Little Nell after the ski slope in Aspen. From that comes her nickname, Nellie. She is the kind of dog that just makes you smile to see her. She has helped me get through lots of lonely nights. She is my companion, my friend. What would we do without our animals?

And there was M.A.—Mary Ann Schiller was her name. I met her one evening in Aspen at a birthday dinner we had with a group of local women. I liked her right away. She was funny, bold, and outspoken. She said exactly what was on her mind and I liked that. She was divorced at the time. She had four children and we ended up talking a lot about our families. I had never met anyone who had the kind of open and close friendship with her children that I had with mine. The more we talked, the more we realized that we had indeed raised our families with similar values—trust, respect, and equality. We laughed as we thought of our children all meeting each other one day, because we knew that they, too, would immediately recognize the similarities in their upbringing. They all did meet. Recognition of the same family values was instant. Today, we all spend holidays together as often as possible. M.A.'s friendship and love was a turning point in my life. I smiled again.

Chantal Westerman is a beautiful and successful television personality I met while with Martina. She could easily have remained Martina's friend and said adios to me. She did not. She is strong. She has a real sense of self. She had the courage to stay beside me when, for obvious career reasons, it would have been more advantageous for her to "ride the white horse."

Chantal and I experienced a mutual "heart-touching," as I call it, one year when Martina and I were in L.A. for the Virginia Slims tournament. We, as usual, had all of our animals with us. We were staying in a friend's home. One of our dogs slipped under the fence in the backyard and was lost for several days in the canyon. Chantal came over to help in the hunt. Together Chantal and I made our way through the thorny thickets looking desperately for our dog. I missed Martina's matches that day, which was rare. Chantal missed them, too. She could easily have joined the others at the matches, but she did not. She chose to help me in the search. Our dog, Yoni, was found. He was one happy, hungry fellow. Chantal and I found a valuable and enduring friendship. Our values were mutual. She is my friend. I've always believed real friendships must have roots in order to grow. I have found that I have a garden.

Where did all my friends go? The real ones stayed. The new ones became real.

# 13

## Aspen: Life Goes On

I woke up alone, a burning ache in the pit of my stomach. My parents had stayed with me in Aspen for a couple of weeks after Martina left, but their lives had to go on. They returned to Fort Worth. I was truly alone, perhaps for the first time in my life. That may seem odd, as I was forty-five, but it is amazingly true.

It was the longest winter of my life. I had no desire to exist, and existing was all that I was doing. All the dreams of my life with Martina had gone up in smoke, and I was left with the burning question why? I had no concept of who I was or where I was going. I had had the same questions when Ed first left me. Again I had to examine myself and my journey. I felt that bitter, lonely, empty, lost feeling once more. I seemed older, but no wiser. I couldn't imagine my life without her. I just wanted her back, and the only thing that was certain in my life was that she wasn't coming back. I knew that I was a survivor— my past had shown me that—but I also knew I felt no reason or need to survive.

The feelings of depression scared me. I sought help. Martina and I had a mutual friend, Annie Denver. She was also a therapist. I called and asked her if she felt she could see me professionally, hoping that it would not change the texture of our friendship because it meant so much to me. She said she thought we should try, and that if either of us felt the session infringed on our friendship or stymied the therapy, then we would stop. As it turned out, that was one of the best things I ever did for myself. For the first time in my life I addressed issues and choices and dealt with my overwhelming sense of guilt and failure. I had not done this when Ed left me. In retrospect, I know I should have. I had to address my "good girl" syndrome head-on. I was not perfect, by any means, and yet the need never to let anyone know my insecurities or even see me vulnerable was too great a burden. I felt that if I didn't find a way to release myself from that pressure—the pressure to *always* be good—I was never going to be really happy. I needed help. Annie Denver gave me that. She taught me to be nicer to myself, to be more patient. She taught me the necessity of being still. She taught me "not to push the river." To this day we have therapy sessions by phone whenever I feel the need to address my insecurities.

I knew that I needed to get out of the house each day. I needed a reason to get up, get dressed, and do something. Pining away in my gloom and sorrow was not going to get me anywhere. I actually had to make myself play tennis again. I needed to force my body to move because it felt frozen and dead. I started going to the gym and lifting weights. More than once I thought of the irony in the fact that I had lived with one of the most fit persons in the world and not until she left did I start taking the time to take care of myself. Oh, how the lessons began to add up.

Through that bleak winter, Debbie Morris, my friend and a wonderful ski instructor, took me to ski. That was also a kind of therapy. I know how lucky I was to have that available to me, but I'll tell you it took every ounce of energy I had some days just to get my ski boots on. Debbie not only taught me to ski, she taught me many other things as well, such as to appreciate the silence and the calm and to feel the energy of the universe.

It was a time of change and examination for me. I had to mourn the loss, and I had much healing to do. The mountains became my sanctuary.

I sought the compassion of friends. For the first time in my life I allowed them to see me in need. Slowly but surely I began to see that I could survive. I began to emerge socially again with groups of friends. Even when my heart was not in it, I made myself dress and go out. There was a hollowness in my heart, but the tenderness and laughter of my friends began to fill the void.

The house I lived in felt big and empty. The bed we had shared for so many years was a constant reminder of her absence. Pictures of Martina in all her glory and pictures of us during special moments still hung on the walls. I didn't know when I would have the courage or desire to take them down. I knew one day I would have to, for they were merely moments of a past life caught by the single click and frame of a camera.

It took almost a year before I had the courage to take all the pictures off the walls, and there were hundreds. I was alone when I did it. I wanted it that way. I remembered and wept. Walking from room to room was like walking through the pages of tennis history. Intermingled were candid shots of the two of us frolicking in snowdrifts up to our ears or riding double and bareback on a paint pony in the wildflower-splattered fields of our ranch property in Aspen. We had been building a home on that land for almost two years. I never saw it completed. Martina finished it several years later after first trying to sell it. She lives there now. I've never been allowed on the property since shortly after she left. I'm sure I'll never see it again.

Bales in particular had lost a parent and a best friend. He told me once that he didn't know why he didn't get to see her. He said that even though his dad and I were divorced, he got to see his dad, and he just couldn't understand why this was any different. Frankly, neither could I.

Life goes on. Aspen is actually a very spiritual place. There was time for me to reflect. In the off-season there are just eight thousand or so locals in that tiny mining town high in the Rockies. Winter finally disappeared as the snow melted and became roaring, dancing mountain streams and rivers. So was my winter gone. The long, cold, mournful days were greeted with the hope of spring. I had begun to feel stronger. The lawsuit was filed and I was focused on standing up for my rights. I knew the fight would be long and hard, certainly against the odds as well as popular opinion. I knew my strength would have to come from within. It was difficult during those days to stay on track, as I seemed to become despondent and discouraged so easily. Once I was down, it would take all the energy I could muster just to get myself going again. My friends came to my aid.

I remember especially a trip over the mountains from Aspen to Crested Butte across the highest peak on horseback. My friend Mindy Nagel and I went with a couple of guys, Craig and Tim, who were polo pros from Zimbabwe. We had met them one evening in one of the hangouts of the Aspen locals, the Woody Creek Tavern, playing pool. For the trip to Crested Butte, they furnished the horses from the pack of polo ponies they were playing that summer, and we were joined by Craig's brother Duncan. The ride over the peak and down into the little ski town took about six hours, and we stopped midway to enjoy a picnic lunch that I had packed into our saddle bags. There in those mountains I found some peace. Even today when I seek myself, I go to the mountains. When on the ride, the five of us would often stop and just absorb the untouched beauty of the wildflowers blowing in the breeze in the valleys hidden between the peaks. We put our trust in the surefootedness of our ponies as they carried us up and down the narrow paths. The horses, the mountains, these were my roots. I was getting in touch with myself, perhaps for the first time since I was a child. I was aware that I was at last taking the time to find out who I really was.

A long ride on horseback, however, does not usually end without some unexpected twist, and this was to be no exception. With just an hour to go, a strong wind came up and blew Mindy's hat off. She was riding in front of me and the hat flew in my direction. My horse was startled as I pulled one leg out of the stirrup and leaned as far as I could out of the saddle to try to catch the flying hat before it hit the ground. Spooked, my horse took off as if the starting gates had just opened at the Kentucky Derby. I knew it was either jump or be dragged. I jumped. It was a clean move and I landed on both feet running, hat in hand. It was a great trick, but my trusty steed was long gone! The guys, in Wild West fashion, raced after him. They caught him only after he had blazed through a group of novice riders out on a pleasant little horseback ride with their instructor. The screaming and hoof-thundering Mindy and I heard from the distance made us think that they had been attacked by a giant grizzly bear. As we caught up to the group scattered about the field, Mindy on horseback and I on foot, we pulled our hats down over our faces so as not to have to look at their fear-filled glares. We didn't utter a word and they were still too frightened to speak. Up ahead the guys had stopped my runaway horse. I mounted and we rode away in silence until we were out of earshot, then we all broke into laughter that echoed into the hills. If it had been on film it would have looked like a clip from *Cat Ballou*. Laughter is the best medicine, and I went home that evening tired, yet cured for a while.

To help me find answers to why my relationship had come to such an abrupt end, and where in the hell I was going from there, I called Rita Mae Brown. Since she had once been a lover of Martina's, I sought solace in the wisdom she had gained from her exploration of their relationship and breakup. Although their relationship was short-lived, it, too, ended abruptly with Rita Mae given no opportunity for discussion. Talking to her was like holding a mirror in front of my life. She shared with me how she had begun to put the pieces of her life back together. She had spent years being introspective. I knew I had years in front of me. It was a great help to know that I was not alone. I had known Rita Mae for years, having been introduced by Martina. Now, she became my trusted friend. She was generous with her time and invited me to speak with her whenever and as often as I felt the need. My need was great. She was always there. She also was still Martina's friend, and they would speak from time to time about our situation. She acted as a mediator, always encouraging us to settle our differences without attorneys. Much to her credit, I believe it was because of her persistence that we settled out of court.

Rita Mae invited me out to Virginia to visit her, to talk and spend some time riding her horses. She also suggested that I take a polo clinic by a pro at the University of Virginia in late spring. The suggestions were fine. I visited her, but it would be over a year before I took her up on the polo idea. That may be the best gift she ever gave me. I found both my love for horses and the challenge of sport in polo.

Although I was learning to go to my friends when I needed help, I still found it difficult. At times in Aspen I would withdraw into my little cocoon, not wanting to see or talk to anyone. I desired to be alone and I was never good at that. I needed to learn to turn alone time into constructive time rather than destructive time. Instead of feeling sorry for myself I needed to get in touch with my feelings and to stay with those emotions even though they were painful. Eventually I would learn that those feelings would not kill me.

One such alone time was an evening at home in Aspen. I had been to town to get some groceries. When I returned, I couldn't find my cat, Lancelot. I looked frantically in all of his favorite hiding places. He was gone. I had raised Lance from a kitten and he was seven years old. I had kept our two cats, Lance and Jenny, and Martina had taken our dogs. The cats and my dog, Nellie, were my best friends and my sources of comfort in my aloneness.

I began to search outside for Lance. I was scared and crying as I aimlessly wandered the foothills and crevices that surrounded my house. Then in the silence of the night as I tried to fight back my tears, I heard his cry far off in the distance. As I was running to catch up with him, I fell tumbling head over heels into a deep ravine. I twisted my knee severely when I tried to brace myself for the fall and felt something tear inside it. Lance, still running away from me, was as frightened as I. For one brief moment he hesitated in his flight, and I made one last fearful leap for him, pushing upward and forward on just one leg. I reached out in the darkness, arms outstretched, hands grasping for the white figure silhouetted in the moonlight. As I fell to the ground, chest first, securely in my arms was my Lancelot.

I did not notice the pain in my knee or the mass of fluid that had accumulated around it until I was safely inside the warmth of the house with Lance still in my arms. After the trauma of the event passed, I realized that I had probably torn the cartilage in the only good knee I had. My right knee had already been operated on three times. The left knee would need surgery, too. I knew it. I drove myself to Vail the next day to see Dr. Steadman, the doctor who had only months before operated on both of Martina's knees. The surgery was scheduled. I was all alone, really alone. There were lessons to be learned. I was still learning how to take care of myself. I had always taken care of everyone else.

Later that summer, however, came a spiritual turning point in my life. It was one of those moments when you can be among a crowd and yet experience a *oneness*, as if you were totally alone in that isolated, suspended moment in time. There had been other spiritual moments throughout my life, but none so real, so profound, as this one. This moment was a gift of hope. At this turning point I felt one with the universe. I knew there was still hope in my life, that I would and could carry on. Even though I never thought my time with Martina would end, it had. I realized that she had come into my life for special and important reasons. By having chosen to live with and love a woman openly, I was becoming more of the person who I really was. I knew, too, that more of me was yet to come forward. One day I would have my own life, not one hidden behind someone else's. I was learning to become my own person. I was struggling to be free.

The experience happened as I was again on that magnificent journey, on foot this time, from Aspen to Crested Butte. I was with special pals: Mary Ann Schiller and her daughter, Stormy, and my son Eddie. At times the air was so thin that I could barely breathe. Now I had two bad knees, but I was determined to make it over the highest peak. It was both a physical and emotional victory for me.

Amazingly, just as we approached the protection of some giant rocks at the highest peak of the mountain, a strong wind came up and the temperature dropped drastically, and snow began to fall in the summertime. We all hovered together under the protection of the overhanging rocks and sat quietly until the unusual flakes disappeared into the billowy heavens from which they seemed to come. Then, as I stepped over the last rock to begin the climb down the other side of the mountain, I looked down and, much to my surprise, saw beneath me, not rocks and fearful ledges, but instead the most beautiful field of wildflowers that I had ever seen. In every color in the rainbow, they stood as high as my waist. It took my breath away. Tears filled my eyes. God had filled my soul with the most beautiful bouquet that I had ever seen. I stood in awe of the most peaceful place my eyes had ever beheld. I was supposed to be there. I was supposed to be with my son. I was supposed to be with Mary Ann.

I walked alone into the field of flowers as the others sat on the ground to enjoy the peace and the calm and the beauty. As I stood there in those flowers, I knew that I wanted one day to have my ashes scattered among them, there in that beautiful field, protected by those majestic mountains. I stood and I experienced peace as I had never known it before. I walked out of the flowers and put my arms around my son and asked him to carry out my wishes. With tears in his eyes he made me that promise.

Life goes on, but as Eddie had said to me many years ago, "it would never be the same." My life would never again be as I thought it would be. What I knew from that moment, just as Eddie had realized years before, was that somehow, someway it would be better. I thank Martina for opening the door that allowed the real Judy Hill Nelson to walk through. I was not there yet, but I was on my way.

There were still other questions to answer in my search. There were more choices to be made.

# 14

## Choices Again: Men or Women?

Did Judy Nelson want to be with a man or a woman? I now had to address that question. Was my life and seven-year love affair with a woman just a fluke or was I truly a lesbian? What was my heart saying?

My parents and my family, I think, wished they could have made that decision for me, or at least influenced it. But I had gone too far down the road in my search for my own soul to turn back now. I wanted to make my own choices, not have them dictated to me by the influences of family or society. I wanted to know my heart and give it its wings. I was certain that I would be happy with the person I had become no matter what the choice.

The obvious and easiest thing to do was to slip quietly back into heterosexuality. That idea was referred to often by my family as "find a good man to take care of you." Somehow, after all those years of accepting me as a lesbian, they were playing those same records again. It sounded like a Garth Brooks song if I ever heard one.

One evening Bales called me in Aspen. Phone conversations with both my sons had always been part of our daily routine.

The calls seemed to help keep the family closer together when we were miles apart. Martina had been gone almost a year, and everyone in the family had finally decided that she was never coming back. They had also decided that I had to start dating and trying to start a new life. They sort of beat around the bush about it, but I got the message. Especially that evening when Bales said, "Mom, why don't you just settle down, forget all this stuff, and find a decent man to take care of you." He truly had my best interests at heart, but I couldn't believe what he had just said to me. Certainly not after all those years, all those talks, all that we had been through together. Deep down inside I knew he must know my heart by now. I was almost angry that he had suggested it, but actually I knew I was just frustrated that he still didn't get the message that I really wanted to be able to take care of myself. It was crucial for me if I was ever going to grow into the person I wanted to be.

I said, "Bales, I can't believe that you just said that. Surely, what I have said and done and stood for in these past seven years has been worth something. Has the message I've been sending been that unclear?" He said, "Mom, you know I understand all your issues, but I just want things to be a little easier for you and I know it's been really tough. It's just an easier way to live, you know that. It would be easier on all of us if you lived with a man again. Anyway, I'm not the one who said it first. Ma [my mother] is the one who said it to me. Maybe you better call her and get on her case, not mine!" He went on to say that in his heart he really did understand my issues and that he, too, wanted to marry a woman who could take care of herself, although he was quick to point out that he wouldn't marry her unless he could "take care of her financially." I knew we, as women, still had far to go in getting our point across. I knew that first we had to believe it ourselves.

After the conversation with Bales, I picked up the phone and called my mother. I confronted her with what Bales had told me, and she agreed that she had indeed made that statement.

She went on to say that she really just wanted me to be happy and felt that life had dealt me a difficult hand. She just wanted things to be a little easier for me. I told her I had to follow my heart. Once more she tried to understand. Once more I felt we had taken three giant steps backward.

They were right about one thing. I needed to start dating people again. I made up my mind to try. I even thought I should date some men just to see if that was an option. That may seem an odd way to put it, but the reality was that Martina was the only woman I had ever been with, and although that was the most fulfilling relationship I had ever had to that point, a tiny part of me wondered if I was angry with *all* men because Ed had been unfaithful. The idea seemed ludicrous to me, but still there was a slight doubt, and I thought I owed it to myself and my family to find out.

A friend suggested that I meet a local fellow that she liked a lot named Philippe Jacquot. She arranged for us all to go to dinner and the movies one night. It was a nice evening and Philippe was charming. He was French and had lived in Aspen only a few years. He was cheerful and very positive. He was also sensitive and loved animals. All those things I liked. It was easy to like Philippe. I was curious as to how it would feel to kiss a man romantically for the first time in so many years. We kissed good night on that first date. He was a "good kisser," as we used to say in high school. But there was no thrill there, no excitement in the kiss. It was just a kiss. Philippe was a prince of a man, but he was not my prince. He never questioned my sexuality. He, of course, knew that I'd been with a woman, but it didn't seem to matter to him. That was as it should be, I thought. I do, even now, wonder why people make such an issue of relationship choices. One must follow one's heart. That is special and sacred—it's about trusting your heart to know how you will be happiest.

Philippe and I became close friends. I had never really had a male friend, so it was all the more special to me. We spent a lot of time together during my remaining year in Aspen. We went to movies, worked out together, and took hikes. He was a Realtor and sold my house for me when I was ready to leave Aspen. Best of all, Philippe made me laugh again. He's back in France now and I hope to see him again one day.

In the meantime I was doing things with my girlfriends, but I was not attracted to them sexually. I think I was open to dating a woman; I just hadn't met one who made my heart skip a beat. Not yet anyway. I did accept a dinner invitation one evening with a woman I worked out with at the Aspen Club. I didn't know if she was gay or straight. I just didn't have that "gaydar" as referred to by some in the gay community. After dinner I took her to her car, as we were in mine. When we stopped, she turned and kissed me on the mouth. I was so startled. I just had not expected it. It frightened me. I wanted this person as my friend, not as my lover. She had crossed some boundary with me. I was mad. That was my first *real* kiss from a woman other than Martina. I was not happy about it.

It surprised me that I felt it was acceptable for an eligible man who had romantic intentions to kiss me, but a woman kissing me who had the same intentions made me uncomfortable. Boy, did I have a lot to learn. This dating thing was not going to be a walk in the park. I didn't know how to date women. I was totally uncomfortable. I was realizing that I had no desire to be with a man sexually. I missed being with a woman. That was becoming more and more apparent to me. I addressed all these issues and feelings in my therapy with Annie.

Yet, I still wanted to see if I could have romantic feelings for a man, because as my family had said, it would be so much easier on everyone. I decided to call a guy I had known for years. I had met him when Ed and I were separated. I was attracted to him, but he was married and I wouldn't touch that with a ten-foot pole. I happened to see him in Aspen skiing over the Christmas holidays. He was as likable and as handsome as ever. He told me that he was divorced and had moved to California several years prior. He knew from all the publicity surrounding our breakup that Martina and I were no longer together, and he suggested that whenever I felt like it to call and he would come back to Aspen to visit me. Several months later I called. It was good to hear his voice. We agreed on a date and he flew out to visit. I met him at the airport. We hugged and then we kissed. It was a good kiss, but it was not her kiss.

He stayed for almost a week. We enjoyed dinners and movies and working out together. He had a great body. I really liked the person he was. He was a good father, spent a lot of time with his kids, and talked about them with great affection. That was important to me. He knew my sons. I also liked that. He was creative in business, always developing his own enterprises. We had that in common. It didn't matter to him that I had been with a woman. He had a lot of respect for Martina. There was so much between us that had value. Yet something was missing—a piece of my heart. I knew it from the first evening. He knew it, too. He was understanding and patient. We spoke openly of my lack of sexual desire. He kept his ego intact. I was glad of that. He was wise enough to know that this was not about him. The very first night he was with me, I asked him if he wanted a separate bedroom or if he wanted to share mine. He said he would love to sleep with me. I told him that would be fine, but that I didn't know what to expect. He was already in the bed when I came out of the bathroom. I slipped under the covers. I felt strange. Sleeping with a man seemed like another life entirely. We began to kiss, and as the kisses

became more passionate, I realized that was all that was going to happen. I wanted to be held in his strong arms. I wanted him to kiss my forehead and cheeks and eyelids, but I did not want to make love with him. I felt safe with him, safe enough that I could tell him of my feelings, or lack of them. He understood. He held me all night long. He held me all the nights to come. When he left, I knew that I wanted to be with a woman one day. I just prayed that one day I would be open enough to let someone into my heart again.

Shortly thereafter I planned a little getaway vacation with five of my best girlfriends. I had not been anywhere since Martina left except once to Texas and once to Virginia to have talks with Rita Mae. Those trips were more or less for therapy. This trip was entirely for pleasure.

After I returned, I felt more positive, more rested. I had the overwhelming feeling that one day my heart could sing again. I allowed myself to really open up with my friends. I was willing to let them see the not-so-perfect me. It felt good. They loved me anyway. I also found I was much more receptive to having a relationship with someone. I was less guarded and tense. The pain of having lost my lover was beginning to subside.

Over the months ahead I found two women to whom I was physically attracted. I knew both had been with women before, but I also knew that both wanted and needed to be with a man. The important thing, I recognized, was that at least I was looking and feeling something again. There was hope.

I found that a single woman could get herself into some rather interesting if not comical situations. Once, one evening I had gone to a club to dance. My sons and my good friend Mindy were among the group. We were all standing in a corner trying to hear each other speak as the music was extremely loud. Finally giving up on trying to converse, we all decided to dance. I was unquestionably the oldest in the group and was left standing with a young man half my age. He was rather obnoxious and had been boasting about his expertise as a skier. Realizing that we were alone, he asked me to dance. I said yes, as I would rather do anything than listen to what we used to call his "bullshit." That was never very ladylike terminology, but I was rapidly loosing my patience with this fellow. He bought us a couple of drinks at the bar and carried them onto the dance floor for us, something

I deplored. However, everyone seemed to be doing it, so I guessed it was a generational thing.

We danced until the music stopped, then he asked if I wanted to join him as he got us another drink. I said no, that I would just wait for him on the dance floor. At least I could have a moment free from him. I would have left long before, but Eddie and Bales were with me and they seemed to be having a good time. Upon his return he had a couple of beers and two shots of tequila. (I'd been known to do shots of tequila because they go down fast, and I don't drink much, nor do I particularly like the taste of alcohol.) I drank one of the shots and then while he wasn't looking, poured the other one on the floor.

All the while Eddie was dancing with his girlfriend right beside us. He kept looking at me, trying to say something, but it was inaudible with the music blasting in our ears. He kept moving closer and closer to me as he danced, never letting me out of his sight. Finally the music stopped again and he moved ever so close and whispered in my ear, "Mom, be careful, you don't know what this guy is trying to do. For God's sake, don't drink any more shots." I told him that I was a big girl who could take care of herself and not to worry. He never left my side the entire evening.

When we all left the club, sans Mr. Cool, Eddie told me the whole story. Apparently, the boastful young man had seen Eddie and me talking earlier in the evening, before the dancing started. When he saw Eddie at the bar during a band break, he went up to him and offered to buy Eddie a beer. He asked Eddie if he knew me very well. Eddie decided to play along with the guy and said, "Sure do. Matter of fact I know her *really* well." With that replay, the young man asked, "Well, is she good to go?" Eddie replied, almost dropping the beer just handed to him, "Guess you'll have to find that out for yourself." Immediately realizing what he had just set his mother up for, Eddie raced to the dance floor and never let me out of his sight.

We all laughed until we hurt because the joke was actually on the young man, who had no idea that I was Eddie's mother!

After we stopped laughing, I asked Eddie why in the world had he not come to my defense with the guy and protected my virtue? He simply replied, "Well, Mom, he was buying me beers, so I wasn't going to punch him out." Eddie also said he thought it was kind of funny until he realized that the guy had every intention of getting me drunk. That's when Eddie got scared. We all laughed again. There was no way Eddie could have known that I must have faced that same situation at least a hundred times when I was in college. I had known a lot of Mr. Cools. To this day, my nearest and dearest friends who know that story call me Good to Go. Mr. Cool did find out several days later that I was Eddie's mother. We saw him in town having dinner with a group of friends. He got up, walked over to us, and apologized profusely. That changed my image of him just a little, for it was a humbling confession.

Examining the lighter side of the question of the choice between men and women, I recall an interview I did with Howard Stern. He had invited me twice to be interviewed on his radio talk show before I finally accepted. I decided that to be interviewed by Howard would be a real challenge. You know you're not ever going to come out ahead of him, but I wanted to just go in there and see if I could keep up with him. I hope I kept up, but I'll tell you, I was running as fast as I could! At one point he said that he thought that perhaps I was a lesbian because I just hadn't had a good man. My retort was that perhaps *he* hadn't had a good man. He laughed and agreed. We were off on the right foot and I had fun sparring with him. He's really a pretty good guy. He must be doing something right. He has a lot of listeners.

On the more serious side of the question of would I be with a man or a woman, the answer came in loud and clear. I had experienced a wonderful relationship with a woman, and again my heart was telling me that that was my desire. There is no fault or blame to be laid. I was not seeking to be with a woman because my husband had been unfaithful. Nor was I seeking shelter with women because of any deeply harbored fears toward men. I was not choosing to be with a woman to be rebellious. Nor was I choosing to be with a woman because I was emotionally disturbed or had some defect from birth. I was as normal as any human being. I was simply expressing what my heart felt. I do not believe that the heart is gender specific. I just don't think it matters when you come right down to it. What matters is what makes the heart sing. If the song it sings does not hurt anyone and does make the singer happy, then how can anyone rightfully or righteously ask us to march to a drum we do not hear?

One may ask, what do I feel when I speak of falling in love with a woman? And how is it different from loving a man? My experience is that on an emotional level it is not different. The feelings of falling in love and of being in love are the same. Some may beg to differ. I have no quarrel with that because as long as we are allowed to be individuals, we will all experience life and loving in different ways. This is simply my account, my life, my feelings. I do not pretend to project those onto anyone else. Aside and apart from the obvious physical differences between men and women, I think it is safe to say, in the words of the old song my daddy used to sing:

> *A kiss is still a kiss,*
> *A sigh is just a sigh.*
> *The fundamental things apply.*

That song was even before my generation, yet the words still ring true. In my experience, a heterosexual relationship and a homosexual relationship are alike as far as emotions are concerned.

I believe that we all want to be true to our hearts. I believe that we should be able to be that anywhere, anyplace, anytime. Peace and loving must first come from within, then they will show on the outside. Real loving and caring for someone, be it in a heterosexual or homosexual way, is never a blatant act; it is a tender one, shared and witnessed primarily by the people involved. The testimony to one's love for another, no matter what kind of relationship, is found in the eyes, the look, and it need not be explained. It simply is.

My choice, having experienced both sides of the fence, so to speak, was again to be with a woman. Today, when I think of the woman I'm now with and love, I feel the bond is greater; the touch softer; the kisses somehow sweeter; the eyes more revealing; the emotions more heartfelt; the hands more soothing; the laughter more endearing; the wit more spontaneous; the gentleness more seductive. If this is what I feel, then I must deduce that I am truly a woman who has loved and does love a woman. Put a label on it if you wish, and if you do, then know, too, that I am happy to be a lesbian.

# 15

## Rita Mae Brown:
## A Couple of What?

Sometimes the best teachers are the hardest ones. Rita Mae was a hard teacher. More than once I've heard her say, "My motto is, 'Revenge is a dish best eaten cold.'" I came to know Rita Mae Brown, perhaps as intimately as anyone had. I lived with her for two years on Tea Time Farm in Virginia. *Intimately*, however, is a contradiction when it comes to knowing Rita Mae. There was no intimacy in our relationship. That is perhaps the single most crucial reason why we could never last as lovers. Thank goodness we both had the sense to realize that we would be much better as friends.

Believe me, no one said it better than Rita Mae herself when she said, "Judy, you better try to remain my friend, because you sure don't want me as your enemy." She was absolutely right.

One may be curious how I ended up in Virginia with Rita Mae. In retrospect there were so many reasons. I still needed and wanted someone in my life. I wanted love and attention again. I suffered when Martina left me. Rita Mae, too, had suffered when Martina left her. We had that in common. She had already proven a valuable friend in helping me get through some rough times during that struggle.

Some people think it odd that two ex-lovers of Martina's should get together. I think it not odd at all. We certainly had much more in common than just Martina. People also think, "It's one of those lesbian things; you know how they just sort of recycle." I laugh when I hear things like that, as if it were just a homosexual pattern. The fact is that it is just as common for an ex-lover of one person to get together with the ex-lover of another in the heterosexual community. Besides, up to that point in my life, I still did not know many available lesbians.

We had many other important things in common. We loved the land and mountains and our animals. We loved horses. She appreciated my ability to feel comfortable in almost any social situation. She liked my Southern good manners. She told me she knew that I was a hard worker, that I was fair and loyal, that I had a real sense of commitment, that I was willing to always do my share and that at times I even had a sense of humor—the most important thing of all, she felt.

Much to her credit, a sense of humor is perhaps her best quality, and is, I believe, what has made her such a popular and enduring writer. She has a quick wit. I liked that. She is extremely bright and very well read. I learned a lot from her. She knows exactly what she wants and is willing to both work for it and wait for it.

When I went to live with Rita Mae, I knew all of those things about her. However, I had yet to learn and experience many things that were not immediately visible—things that would ultimately drive a wedge between us.

Some reasons why I went to live with Rita Mae were unconscious. I didn't want to be hurt again. I didn't ever want to be left again. I thought she was a perfect choice. She takes great pride in her word. If she gives you her word on something, you can count on it. I believed her. I knew that if she gave me her word that she would not leave, she wouldn't. I knew if she said she would be faithful, she would.

Again, hindsight is usually the most perceptive sight of all, and I realize now that I should have given myself more time alone after Martina left. A year and a half was not enough. I needed to experience life all alone, something I had not ever really done. Being with Rita Mae was often lonely, but I still was not alone. There is a subtle difference. The difference is immense, however, for one's personal growth. I had chosen my new path. I would learn the lesson I needed in another way. My patterns seemed to be much the same: to love and live with someone powerful and be the person working behind the scenes. I was taught that was the woman's place, and although I fought the concept with all my might, it continued to influence my relationships. I'm a firm believer that you go through life getting the same messages, just wrapped in different packages, until you finally get the lessons. With Rita Mae the messages came through loud and clear, and some difficult lessons were learned.

For a while her unemotional approach to relationships was just what I needed. I still had some grieving to do. She knew it and was willing to let me do it. I think she grew tired of my grieving at her expense, as it took up time and kept me from moving forward. I think she grew bored with my self-indulgence. I don't blame her. Even I grew tired of it, but I just couldn't make myself progress through the lessons I had to learn. I just kept hitting walls head-on.

She was one tough teacher, but to grow I needed such a taskmaster as she. I had a lot of admiration for her—still do. My greatest lesson, however, was to realize firsthand that I didn't want to be like her. That is not to say that I don't respect her, for I do. Yet, I realized once more that I am a "hands-on" kind of person. That emotional part of me is still an extremely important part of my identity. Rita Mae is the opposite. She is fine as long as you leave her alone and give her lots of space. She decided early in her life that she didn't want to need anybody. Therefore, the painful reality was that she could never give me what I needed—someone to hold me and touch me and physically need me. I thought, when going with her, that I wanted to do away with that part of me, for it was that emotional and loving person that always seemed to get hurt. I never wanted to hurt in such a deep, emotional way again. I thought I could live without romance and passion. I thought that I could put all of that energy into my love of the mountains and land and horses. She had. I wanted to learn how she had done it.

I did learn, but as it turned out, I didn't want to pay the price: to never, ever need anyone or give myself to anyone again. She had mastered the art of shutting out emotions if they got in her way.

The longer I lived with Rita Mae, the more I realized that the emotions, the passions, the romance that I felt had to be expressed, not repressed. By observing Rita Mae, I learned how I didn't want to be. That is not to say that Rita Mae lacked emotion or passion. She could not write the way she does and be so successful without them. It is just that she channels all of that energy into her books, into her characters, on the page. I think it must be safer there, for one has control of it.

When I moved to Virginia in late spring of 1992, a year and a half after Martina had left, the only thing I wanted to be in control of was my own life. I set about doing that ever so cautiously. I didn't want to share my thoughts or ventures with anyone. That was a mistake, for Rita Mae was a wise adviser and I sought to close myself off from her advice. I did so want to be my own person. I didn't want to be the person *behind* someone else ever again. Nor did I want to take care of matters for anyone again to the extent that I actually was in control of his or her life.

Judy Nelson had a lot of growing to do, and Tea Time Farm with Rita Mae Brown was just about the best place to do it, I was convinced. Rita Mae must have thought so, too, because after many talks, she invited me to be her partner, financially, in the farm that she holds so dear. That may prove to be the only wise decision I made financially.

Tea Time Farm was an animal lover's paradise. The Blue Ridge Mountains, the rolling pastures, the wild foliage, the abundance of native trees, the dogwoods in springtime, and the rich palette of colors in the fall—all created a place where God would want to live on earth. It was peaceful. It was spiritual. It provided the atmosphere needed to heal my broken heart. Rita Mae sensed this need and was kind enough to make me the offer. On the other hand, I could help *her* if the partnership worked. Two could always do twice as much as one. With me as her partner in the farm, she could realize her dreams twice as fast and with only half the output in cash and energy.

The only question that remained was, could the two of us actually live together as lovers? In the beginning I had only an inkling that the definition of *lovers* meant very different things to us. I remember when a friend of mine asked Rita Mae where she would most like to make love and had yet never experienced. She replied without blinking an eye, "Inside a bank vault, on top of all that money." Yes, we were different people.

It would take exactly two years for Rita Mae and me to learn that we were much better friends than lovers. Near the end of our relationship, during discussions about my emotional needs, Rita Mae would often declare that I was self-centered and egotistical. I at least understood where she was coming from when she made those accusations. For the first time in my life I was willing to talk about needs in a relationship. I think this willingness to confront translated into selfishness to Rita Mae. I was continually expressing that my emotional needs were not being met.

In late spring of 1994, I took my empty emotional bags but also my bags filled with newfound wisdom given to me by a good teacher, and I left Tea Time Farm. I did not know where

I was going or what I was going to do. I did know the things about me that I liked and wanted to keep, and that was more than I knew coming into the relationship.

During my years with Martina I had been very removed from the lesbian community, and the same was true while I was on the farm with Rita Mae. Not until 1993, when *Love Match* was published, did I begin to meet and get involved with the lesbian community. At that point I began to realize that I felt strongly about gay and lesbian issues and that I was no longer going to remain silent about them. I knew I had something to say and that I certainly had an interesting perspective, having been completely heterosexual for most of my life. I knew that if anyone wanted to listen, I was more than willing to share my experiences. This time I was speaking in my own voice and not expressing views and experiences through someone else. It felt good. Rita Mae encouraged me to have my own voice and challenged me to write this book. I believe she is especially good at unselfishly helping people be the best that they can be. I think she did that for Martina as well. She encouraged Martina to use her brain for something other than just tennis. Through Rita Mae's encouragement, I think, Martina grew to have an even greater love of books and learning and developed a vocabulary superior to that of most Americans. Hats off to you, Rita Mae.

So where did I go wrong again? That's always my first thought—the thought that I have failed, for that is the way I was taught. The older I get the more I realize that because my relationships with Ed, Martina, and Rita Mae did not last, I did not necessarily fail. I did grow from each of those relationships, learning what I did want for my life and in a relationship and what I didn't want.

What happened with Rita Mae? When asked once if we were a couple, I would ask in response, "A couple of what?" She was and is her own person; I was desperately trying to be my own person, and the two of us just didn't fit. We couldn't know that until we lived together for a while. In the beginning, as with most lovers, homosexual or heterosexual, the time taken to get to know each other was exciting. There was time for kissing and lovemaking, and for rides on horseback. As time marched on, however, I realized that only the horseback-riding time was essential to Rita Mae. I wanted and needed the romantic aspects of the relationship to continue. That was and *is* extremely important to me. It was way down on Rita Mae's list. Lovemaking for me is about intimacy. For Rita Mae, I think, it was merely about having fun. And that for me was not fulfilling; thus we drifted further apart. I began to feel that she wanted me as an ornament. She would like me to get all dressed up when we were going to an important social function that might prove financially or politically advantageous, and she would ask me to "work the room." I didn't like the way I felt when she expressed this. I felt as if I were back in college during rush week, trying to impress the young girls so that they would pledge our sorority.

From the very beginning some signs made me doubt if we really could live together. For instance, I never had any of my clothes in our master bedroom. I was also relegated to the basement. She explained that she had built the house for herself, not thinking of having a permanent mate. Odd, I think, because Rita Mae, like Martina (and myself), usually has someone in her life if not in her house. Maybe if she puts you in the basement, it makes it easier to move you out without too many traumatic changes. Anyway, I never felt a part of that house, even though I was paying half the mortgage each month. I also was paying for half the land and upkeep of the farm, but it was never, not even by our closest friends in Charlottesville, referred to as *our* farm. It was Rita Mae's farm. You would have thought by then I would be getting tired of that. I think in the end I was dead tired of it.

She did offer me a couple of drawers in the bathroom. It had two sinks. After a few weeks of trying to bathe and do makeup upstairs and then run downstairs to get my clothes, or vice versa, I gave up on the invitation and began using the bathroom in the basement as well.

She had a wonderful, cozy library-office upstairs. I shared an open-space office in the basement with one or two other people whom she employed. All notices or deliveries were made at the basement door as per instructions on a sign at the front entrance of the house. No one was ever to knock at the front door for it would distract from her writing. She could lose a word, a sentence, a thought, if disrupted. I understood this, but at times a bitterness arose that my work should be deemed any less important. In reality it probably was, but it still didn't make me feel any better.

She offered to add on to the house as well as to build an entirely separate office for her. The offer was nice, but she wanted me to pay for the additions to the house. She would pay for the office. I had no money to add anything to anything. I was struggling each month just to keep up with the mortgage and the farm expenses. She knew this. And even if she built a new office, she never offered to give me her old one. I would still be in the basement, and her existing office would become a lovely library–sitting room. It was clear to me that Tea Time Farm would never be *ours*. I owned half of it, but it was *hers*, always would be.

Just in case I wasn't really sure about that fact, she back-handedly let me know. I had been gone on a business trip to Texas for about ten days. When I returned, she was not at the airport to meet me as planned. I called. She said that it was beginning to snow at the farm, which was some thirty minutes out of Charlottesville. She said that she was afraid the weather would only get worse, and she was not going to drive in it. She advised me to get a cab and go to the nearest hotel until the storm subsided. I told her that the roads in town were perfectly clear and that I just wanted to get home. It had been a long trip. We had four-wheel-drive vehicles and I assured her that it would be no problem. I was used to lots of snow, having lived in Aspen for three years. The conversation was not going any-where. Nothing I said was going to convince her that it was safe to drive. I tried to rent a four-wheel-drive car, but there was no such animal in Charlottesville. I called the Ford dealer, a friend, and asked if he could loan me a jeep or Explorer. He had nothing available. He offered to come to the airport and give me a lift in his jeep. I said no, but he insisted. He took me to the farm. The roads were fine. I was disappointed that Rita Mae would not even make the effort, especially since we hadn't seen each other for a while. But we were different that way.

After the friend left, I started down the stairs to the basement to put my things away. The first thing I realized was that many of my pieces of furniture were missing from the living room and sitting room. All of my accessories had been removed from the tabletops. I felt this was the final blow. We were no longer mak-ing love on any regular basis, and it was often weeks between kisses. I was shriveling up emotionally, and now I felt that I had bodily been removed from the house. Nothing was left of my things to be seen. Startled and angry, I asked where my furnish-ings were. She replied that she thought that they cluttered the house and she had put some things in the hayshed and some in one of the horse trailers until they could be moved to storage.

Talk about a message. I got it. It was not subtle. It was a di-rect blow to the head. Likewise, I was alarmed, because a few of the pieces were quite nice and made of lacquer. They would be damaged by the cold temperatures outside. The temperature had already dropped to well below freezing, and no one could guess how long the approaching storm would last. I told her this and asked that she help me move those pieces into the basement until we could decide what to do with them. She agreed to help.

In the cold of the night we went to the horse trailer where I found my lacquer coffee table. The marble top of the table was broken into pieces. I felt as though I were going to throw up. I could barely get out the words: "What happened?" She told me that they had dropped it carrying it out of the house. She said she was sorry and that she would have it replaced. I knew it could not be replaced. It was an original piece made by Memphis. The only other piece like it is in the Museum of Modern Art in Manhattan. My heart was broken as well. She never replaced or repaired the marble top. I still have the pieces. The table was just an object, but I was not. A bit of me had been damaged. The end of our relationship was near. That was the winter. I left Tea Time Farm in the spring. Rita Mae wasted no time in replacing me. I met her and her new lover coming in the driveway to the house as I was pulling out in my pickup truck with the last of my belongings.

There had been conflict even before the episode with the furniture, however. Early on, I wanted to invite friends and especially family to the farm to visit. I was informed that it was fine as long as we agreed on a time, but more importantly, arranged a place where they could stay. I didn't understand this. They, of course, would stay at our home. "No, they cannot," was the reply. If she did not know the guests, I understood. But the fact that my sons were not welcome to stay with us was beyond my comprehension. She explained that they made too much noise and there was not enough room. I told her they were grown boys and would be quiet. We had a guest room and beds could be made on couches in the basement. She refused my suggestions. Upon visits, I reserved rooms in nearby bed-and-breakfasts for friends and family. Only my parents and special, close mutual friends were allowed to stay in the house. I didn't like this mind-set. It did not feel comfortable.

I remember the time Eddie and Bales and their girlfriends came to visit (not sleeping in the house, of course). Eddie had to write a paper for one of his law courses before returning to class on Tuesday. He asked Rita Mae's assistant if he could use the computer to write it. Eddie spent the next four hours putting the essay into the computer. Earlier I had invited Rita Mae down to watch a movie with us while Eddie wrote his paper, but she declined. She said she would stay upstairs and read. I thought that was a bit rude, as she had not even come downstairs to offer hello and welcome the boys and their friends to the farm.

I cooked dinner for all of us and went to the bedroom to invite Rita Mae as well. She said she had already had a snack. Obviously, she wanted nothing to do with the visitors and was unhappy that they were in the house.

After dinner, the kids went back to the basement to continue watching the movie while Eddie finished his paper. They had been careful to turn off all the lights and the television just as I had instructed. Eddie had, however, left the computer on because he did not know how to save his essay. Just after they had returned downstairs, I heard loud, angry footsteps pounding back up the stairwell, as if someone were taking four steps at a time. Eddie, all six feet four inches of him in his heavy cowboy boots, was in a rage. He first accused me of turning off the computer. I said I had not. He raged even more. He had lost his entire essay because the computer had been cut off. Together we went back downstairs, and looking under the desk, I saw that all the plugs had been pulled out of the sockets. Now I was angry. Wanting some explanation, I ran upstairs to ask Rita Mae if she had pulled the plugs. She was nowhere to be found. I didn't know what to think. Now I was more concerned about her. Finally, I walked down to the barn, the only place I hadn't looked. I found her asleep on the floor of the tackroom. I woke her and asked her what was going on. She said that the lights and the sounds from the basement had been keeping her awake. While we were eating, she had gone to the basement because she could hear the buzzing from the computer. That plus the electricity being wasted were driving her crazy. She pulled the plugs. I told her in distress that she had erased Eddie's entire paper and that he would have to start completely over. I do not believe that she intentionally erased his essay. She could not have known that would happen. She had, however, made her unhappiness clear. I learned from this that Rita Mae would probably never share my views on family nor did I think she would ever be able to share herself with me.

I asked her if we could see a therapist together, something neither Ed nor Martina had been willing to do. After some insistence she finally agreed. From that counseling we realized that we would probably need to learn a "third language" because, when it came to emotions, we spoke different ones. Neither of us could understand the other. We realized also that we would probably never learn that necessary language. From that we decided that we needed to go our separate ways. Again I had a hard time accepting the decision because it was always taught that if two people agreed to live together and could not, they had failed.

But the most valuable lesson I learned from this therapy was the art of being still. I had never realized how important that was. I was actually afraid of stillness and had no tools for attaining it. Dr. Sharon Beckman Brindley, our therapist, opened that door for me. Inside I found a calmness in my soul. At first I was afraid of it. In it I was vulnerable. But after practice I realized that I would not die if I chose not to always act upon my fears in an attempt to exert some control over them. I realized that the fear and panic would actually subside if I would just be still. I was changed.

Although Rita Mae and I did not stay together, I realized that she did share with me her most treasured possessions: her farm, her horses, her dogs, her cats, and her knowledge. For all that I am eternally grateful.

She also shared a dream with me and together we made it come true: Old Blue, a Sports Equestrian Center. This was composed of a fox-hunting club, a polo club, and a place that afforded equestrian events of all kinds, primarily hunter/jumper and cross-country events. It was completed just as I left the farm. We established it on our existing land plus some new acres we acquired for that purpose. After I left, Rita Mae bought back my half of Tea Time Farm. She also bought back all of Old Blue, for it was located on the farmland. At that point, the land had value, not Old Blue. Again I had helped create something. Again I lost it. At least this time I understood why. I knew that it was not wise for me to keep an interest in an enterprise that had not yet accrued any value. I could not own the land upon which Old Blue sat because it was a part of Tea Time Farm.

When I left Tea Time Farm, I felt I needed an attorney. What I had invested in the farm was all I had, and I needed to be certain that it was protected. I had learned some lessons the hard way. I was becoming cautious, if not cynical. It cost both of us thousands of dollars to get an agreement drawn up, and neither of us was happy about that. But I knew that I would rather be certain than sorry. I lost money on the deal in order to keep the peace. In a way I left Rita Mae holding the bag with a huge responsibility to a venture she really didn't have time to run herself, Old Blue. I knew she would be creative and make it all work. She has. She always will. She's good that way. She is a most determined woman. She is also a most patient woman. I like both those qualities.

Thus we, the odd couple, or "couple of what?" parted ways, each, I think, giving and taking something of value. Our friendship remains intact. I chose to remain in Virginia after my two years on the farm with Rita Mae. Occasionally we play polo or go "fox chasing" together. My partner, Kay, goes with me, and Rita Mae's lover is usually present, although she does not ride all that much. I like what little I know of her, and Rita Mae seems really happy. I like that about Rita Mae. She is basically a cheery person. She has taken the hand life dealt her and learned early to always keep an ace up her sleeve. I do not think she will ever again be caught as unaware, emotionally or financially, as she was when Martina left her.

On the lighter side of things, by choosing to remain near Charlottesville, I was invited to join the Rita Mae Brown Exes'

Club. There are quite a few of those women in that town. The idea seemed quite humorous, but I also think that the ladies, much to Rita Mae's credit, consider themselves a select group. I did not really join the club, as I was certain that it was all in jest. But I think the gesture revealed that one of the things Rita Mae's girlfriends had in common (besides most being tall, slender, athletic, and blond) was their sense of humor. That was a prerequisite from the Queen of *Rubyfruit Jungle* (which of course is the hilarious book that made Ms. Brown famous).

Many have suggested that since Martina made a monetary settlement with me Rita Mae only wanted me in order to get some of Martina's money, for she had lost a lot of her own when Martina left her, in a strange twist of fate. If this suggestion is really true, then Rita Mae has surely enjoyed her motto "Revenge is a dish best eaten cold" to the fullest. She got Martina's woman and she got Martina's money. I like to think she thought more of me than that—or maybe there was madness in her method. Only Rita Mae knows.

# 16

# The Argentina Connection: Deceit and Greed

*Do* cry for me, Argentina! Oh, yes, there was a reason to cry. I want to tell the story of my Argentine investment because I learned lessons that I want to share. Simply put, it is the story of how a vulnerable and naïve woman entrusted all the money she had with people she thought were her friends and had only her best interests at heart. It is the story of a woman who seemingly lost everything she had only to find that she had something else, with much more value, that could never be taken away.

When I sold my house in Aspen, I took a portion of my money to become a partner with Rita Mae in Tea Time Farm. I was still not sure what my life's work would be but hoped it would have something to do with horses. Soon after I moved to Virginia, I was invited by a friend and past business partner in the MN Clothing Company, Frank Albero, and his girl-friend, Gloria Burdette, to visit his ranch in Argentina where he stabled his horses. He was interested in selling them to me or shipping them to the United States where I would have them trained and sell them as polo ponies. It seemed like an

With Kay and Dr. Michael Iott

Dad, Mother, and me with Kay in Fort Worth, Texas

Between Bales and Eddie, 1991

Christmas with Bales and Eddie in Fort Worth, 1992

Some selections from my Ford Agency portfolio

COURTESY MICHAEL KEEL

COURTESY JEFF BARK

COURTESY MICHAEL KEEL

exciting and interesting venture. I figured the worst that could happen was that I would see a bit of a country that I had always longed to visit, and I would get to see some real Argentine polo ponies as well as some professional players, if I was lucky. That was not the worst that happened.

Because I had so much to learn about horses, especially polo ponies, I invited a knowledgeable person to go on the trip with me as both friend and adviser. Excited, we hopped on a plane and, many hours later, arrived in Buenos Aires. We were met at the airport by Frank and Gloria. We all greeted each other with smiles as big as Texas. That was then.

Frank had lived in New York for almost twenty years. For as long as I had known him, which was then about four years, he had had a lot of business in his native Argentina. Frank was no stranger. When the clothing company with Martina was viable, my parents went down with Frank to visit some of the textile factories that were producing fabrics we were using. We all thought of him as a friend. As things go, I would have been wiser to heed Peter Johnson's warning that Frank was not to be trusted. During the negotiations between Martina and Frank regarding the clothing company, Peter Johnson, of IMG, had expressed his doubts about Mr. Albero's character because Frank wanted to do business with just a handshake. We signed contracts with him anyway, but we had experts from IMG go over them with a fine-tooth comb. All in all, Frank had always kept his word to me, even though at times he had seemed evasive.

Upon my arrival in Buenos Aires I had expectations of a business venture that would be both lucrative and fun. We saw the ranch. We rode the horses. We ate the local food and drank the local wine. We laughed. In between we talked of business and investments.

As we talked of the cost of getting horses to the United States and how much time it would take, I realized that the venture was not going to be profitable. I was a bit discouraged until the last day of our trip, when Frank said, "Judy, trust me.

I have a friend in business down here and we can get you twenty-four percent interest on your money. You don't have to do anything. We will talk more when you get back to the States, but I promise on my mother's grave I will take care of you and make you a rich woman." The words were just what I wanted to hear. Someone was going to take care of me, but it was going to be *my* decision. My dreams would be answered. I would have security for my sons and myself.

First I needed to find out how my investment could earn 24 percent. Would it be safe? Was it guaranteed? Was it insured? How would I send money to Argentina and how would I get it out of Argentina? How long would my investment be tied up? Could I take the interest periodically and not touch the principal? Frank said that in time he would answer all these questions.

I remember that he asked me how much money I could invest and was very disappointed when I told him. I think he must have believed all the newspaper articles about my supposed fortune. At any rate he said that he would help me. He knew that security was important because I had never been a woman alone before. Frank was the first person in this web of deception.

The second was a man named Jorge DiGiorgio, a resident of Buenos Aires. He was Frank Albero's longtime friend and associate in Argentina. Mr. DiGiorgio would ultimately be the man to whom I wired my money. I sent it straight from my bank to his. It was merely a phone call—quick, easy, and seemingly painless. There was one major problem. That was the last time I would ever see that money. To this date I have not succeeded in retrieving my investment or the interest due.

After my arrival back home I called my accountant in Texas, Dawn Wegner. Dawn had been my parents' accountant for more than thirty years and had even done some accounting for Ed and me when we were married. Dawn had often made suggestions to our family when she knew of sound investments. I felt I could trust her with my money. I hoped she could give me some guidance as to expenditures and savings. I wanted help with a financial plan.

During my phone conversation with Dawn Wegner, I told her of the opportunity Frank Albero had offered that would reap a whopping 24 percent interest. I told her I didn't have much information but that Frank would be in the States in a week and that he had agreed to join me in Texas to meet specifically with her and explain the investment. She agreed to join us. A couple of weeks later the three of us sat in Dawn's office and talked at length about how the investment worked. I was nervous but excited. Dawn listened carefully and asked all the same pertinent questions that I had. After Frank left, Dawn and I discussed the venture further. There were many questions. Dawn agreed to go to Buenos Aires on my behalf and meet with Frank and DiGiorgio. We agreed that I would invest only after she had thoroughly investigated the proposition, the company, and the people involved. I told her that I would rely completely on her findings and advice.

Dawn left the next week. I paid all of her expenses. During that trip, Dawn Wegner created her own business (even registered the company in Argentina while there) with DiGiorgio.

Dawn had gone to Argentina entirely on my behalf to decide whether I should invest in a factoring company owned and operated by DiGiorgio, whom I had never met. I had learned from earlier talks with Frank Albero that factoring was common in Argentina because it was difficult and time-consuming to obtain loans there. Factoring was a quick fix at a high price. Private companies such as DiGiorgio's would find investors to invest cash for the short term, affording them a high interest rate. He would in turn loan that money at an even higher rate to large companies in need of quick cash.

Dawn was to secure documents, check on the legalities, record a history of the company, and make a thorough report on the factoring operations and its owners or partners and other investors. I was told before Dawn went to Argentina that

the investment would be insured. Dawn was to verify the validity of that statement. I was to receive the accrued interest on
my investment by the month. She was to be certain that I could
actually have that as an income until I either created my own
business or found a job I enjoyed. If, indeed, all of these
promises proved legitimate, then she was to advise me how and
where to write my investment. She called me many times from
Argentina about her findings.

Before she returned to the United States, she told me she
was satisfied and requested that I send the funds to Mr. Di-
Giorgio's bank via my bank. I did as instructed. Then I asked
Dawn where the money was actually being placed. She told me
that part of it was being loaned to a large, established whole-
sale-food chain and the other part to a company bottling spring
water, an important commodity in Argentina. Only after inves-
tigation by the attorneys that I hired almost two years later did
I learn the actual distribution of my money: part to the bottling
company owned by DiGiorgio's partner and a percentage to
Frank Albero.

At the time I was to wire the money, one promise made to
me had changed completely and another one was "being
worked out." The first hitch was that I could not get interest
each month as originally promised, but only every three
months. Next, Dawn and DiGiorgio had not completed negotiations with the insurance company that would guarantee the
investment, as there was bickering about the cost of the policy.
She assured me it would be resolved but suggested that I go
ahead and wire the money so that she could be certain it had
arrived and was put in the proper hands before she returned
home. I wired the money and told her again that I would not
be comfortable until it was insured. She then informed me that
Lloyd's of London would be the insurer but suggested that I
rethink the importance of insurance as it would be costly, thus
bringing my returns down. She suggested that she and Di-
Giorgio might even form their own insurance company to in-

sure not only my investment but also the investments of other clients that might be secured when she returned.

Upon her return, I discovered my investment had not been insured, as I had requested, nor could I touch it or my interest until the end of the year's contract, at which time I could reinvest if I wished. I was outraged and told her to demand that DiGiorgio draw up another contract reflecting the original promises. We were informed that the agreement could not be changed. I phoned Frank Albero for help. He agreed the contract could not be changed. Dawn and I had both been deceived.

Now I was furious. I was scared, even frantic. I could do absolutely nothing but wait until the year's contract was up, then get my money as far away from those people as I possibly could. The deception and the fear that I had been the victim of some horrible scam ate at my gut. I tried to ignore the possibility that the venture might be a total loss, but the thought gnawed at me like a vulture eating its prey. I would just have to wait and hope. I kept silently repeating the phrase my mother had taught me almost from birth, "Good things happen to good people." I thought I was a good person, so surely this ordeal would turn out perfectly as promised. There was always the underlying question, however, that if it didn't turn out, did that mean that I was bad? Such simple and childish thoughts. I wondered where all that was coming from. I did *so* want to grow up.

After ten months of living with the fear that I might not get my investment back, let alone the interest due, I began to try to think positively, because the thought of having lost everything was eating me alive. I made calls to Dawn about how the money should be wired to my bank. The due date drew closer and she still had no exact instructions from DiGiorgio; as a matter of fact, she disclosed that she was having difficulty contacting him by phone or fax. I became literally sick. I made frantic, pleading calls to Frank Albero in New York asking for his intervention. He had made commitments in the first place, and I felt he was as responsible as DiGiorgio. He always made himself out to be the guy in the white hat, the one who had only my best interests at heart. What he really had was most of my net worth, which I did not learn until a year and a half after the investment was due and payable.

Upon my relentless insistence, however, Frank arranged a meeting in New York at which he, DiGiorgio, and I were to discuss my repayment. He also assured me that DiGiorgio would bring at least some of the money owed me with him. The meeting took place at the Hyatt Hotel on November 26, 1993, and I got no money. DiGiorgio did agree to meet me in Texas on December 27, 1993, and bring at least some of it then.

Meanwhile, I had hired an attorney in Fort Worth to help me with this matter as advised by my attorneys in Argentina. He attended the meeting in Fort Worth with DiGiorgio and me. I wanted to be certain that everything was being recorded and that I would have proper recourse if DiGiorgio did not produce the money promised and arrange for the payment of the balance due. After eight hours of fragmented Spanish and English conversation, he turned over less than 8 percent of the investment. A conference call was made to one of his partners in Argentina, who guaranteed my attorney and me that another installment on the money owed would be wired to my bank within thirty days. It never arrived.

I have accrued thousands of dollars in attorneys' fees since that date, both in Argentina and in Texas, but to no avail. If I sued DiGiorgio personally, the financial risk was great and the benefits small. He was a citizen of that country and I was not. The odds were in his favor. More frightening was that we found that he had no assets in his name at all. In essence, he had no net worth. Even if I were to win a lawsuit against him, I would have nothing to retrieve. On paper he had no money, property, homes, or cars. Slick. The attorneys also informed me that such a suit could cost thousands more dollars and several years in the courts.

The next option was to file criminal charges against him. I really wanted to do that. I wanted some revenge. I wanted to see DiGiorgio in jail. Again, I was advised that such action would be most costly and could take as long as five years. If I won, he would go to prison, but I would still not have recovered one penny, and it would have cost me money I didn't have.

I even went so far as to investigate the financial holdings of Frank Albero. He had no assets, either in bank accounts or in holdings recorded in his name. Slick, very slick.

My attorneys in Argentina, in one last effort, suggested that I contact my U.S. senator in Texas to get the U.S. embassy in Buenos Aires to take some action against DiGiorgio. Though the embassy would probably not involve itself in a private matter, it might at least request a meeting with Mr. DiGiorgio and perhaps threaten to withdraw his passport privileges if he did not negotiate a payback agreement with me.

I wrote to Kay Bailey Hutchison, the U.S. senator from Texas, twice. I am most grateful for her help and concern. Because of it, the U.S. embassy contacted me personally and met with my Argentina attorneys. As a result, a registered letter was written to Jorge DiGiorgio on my behalf requesting a meeting. He never responded. End of story.

There were lessons learned again, expensive ones. Be patient and thorough in your investigations before handing money over to anyone. As long as the dollars are in your own hands, you are in control. Never invest your money in a country where you do not speak the language—it will ultimately be a major barrier in negotiations. Do not ever gamble more than you can afford to lose. And especially, if it looks "too good to be true," it probably is.

I'm not financially secure, as I hoped, but I have a newfound strength, one that cannot be taken away. It is inside me.

# 17

## Kay: Love at First Sight

It was love at first sight. Every now and again someone walks casually and unexpectedly into your life. It is special. You are changed. Acceptance is clear and unquestioned. It is a gift—always a gift. And so it was with Kay. She came into my life without warning. Kay was my gift.

Little did I know, however, that Kay had been living and working in Paris for nine years when we met. She was visiting her family in Charlottesville and planned to return to Paris in September to resume her work and finish her Ph.D. in English literature from King's College, University of London.

We met in June 1994 on a beautiful, sunny, warm afternoon. A group had gathered at a friend's farm with a polo field. It was one of only a few grass fields in Charlottesville. The farm had developed into a polo club called Alta Mira, and all the horse lovers in the area came out to play what one might call "pickup" games on Sunday afternoons. The best part about the games was that you could come with one pony or with a whole string of ponies, depending on your level of play and devotion to the sport. No matter one's skills, everyone got to play. The laughter and the thundering of hooves from the game could be heard as far off as the neighboring farmhouses.

All were there because they loved sport and competition. All were there because they loved horses.

Kay had come to watch, as do a lot of the local people, especially the horse lovers. Later I would discover that not only was Kay a horse lover, but she could ride like the wind. Seeing her hop on a horse bareback, often without even a halter, makes my heart sing. It is like witnessing the most freeing experience—man, animal, and nature coming together in harmony, totally trusting and fearless. Seeing Kay in those moments makes me the happiest. That is the vision of her I hold the dearest, as if she is some wild but gentle creature calming all the forces of nature with her own innate fearlessness. In later conversations I would even find out how she had traveled around the world alone for many months and, once (in only one of many such adventures), had just hopped on a plane from Paris to Bangladesh when she heard of the victims in the May 1991 cyclone disaster. Kay was fearless. Kay was my calm.

On that Sunday I was focused on the polo match at hand, the preparations for which must be thorough. One's tack and polo gear must be in good condition. The horses, before they are mounted to play, must be examined completely, both for the safety of the horse and of the rider. In polo, safety of the horse is foremost.

As I was going through my checkpoints before mounting, out of the corner of my eye I glimpsed a small, dark-haired, pretty girl in jeans and a sleeveless, white T-shirt. She was walking beside another girl and had a little beagle on a long leash as she came down the gravel road toward the front of the barn—and toward me. Most spectators gathered in that area at the front of the barn around a picnic table. It was usually piled with meats and cheeses, watermelons and tomatoes, to be enjoyed later by both spectators and players as they joked about the near misses or congratulated others for goals actually made. As I watched her for those few moments, it was as though I knew her. She was somehow familiar. Though I had never seen her before, I *knew* her. I wanted a closer look. I walked past her, asking only what her little dog's name was. She said, "It's Lauren." That's all I said to Kay. I bent over to pet Lauren, then continued on my way to finish tacking up my horse for the first chukker (a seven-minute period in polo, of which there are six). I played the rest of the afternoon with all the intensity that the sport demands. I love it for that reason. When I play, I can think of nothing else, lest I get killed or kill someone else!

During the few minutes allowed between chukkers, given in order to get a fresh pony or grab a quick drink of water, I found my mind wondering about that mysterious, lovely, dark-haired girl with the beagle. I would watch her, although not directly so that she wouldn't think I was staring, wondering why she was there, why I had never seen her there before, and with whom she had come. Only later would I find out she was with her sister. Another thought also crossed my mind, as it never really had before with a stranger: Was she straight or gay? It amused me to think that for the first time in my life I was speculating on whether someone was gay. I had usually known which sex the people I met preferred romantically, and if by some chance I did not, the question did not need to be answered because I was not interested in them sexually anyway. But this was different. Kay was different. I found myself actually hoping she liked women, but I had no way of knowing. I wanted to talk to her, and I just knew that I knew her. I had always known her. That was the feeling. Somehow, some way, I wanted to talk to her about this profound sensation.

As luck would have it (or maybe it wasn't luck at all—only Kay can answer that question), she stayed around until after the polo match finished. I remember untacking my couple of ponies, washing them down, and putting them in my friend's trailer to be taken back to her farm until the next polo game. Ever since I left Tea Time Farm, I had boarded my horses with a friend at a nearby stable. I was never going to give up that part of my life again—my life with my horses—if I could help it.

I strolled over to the picnic table, hot, sweaty, and dirty, to join in the camaraderie and food. I could always learn something new about the game as I sat there chatting with some of the guys who had been playing polo since they were kids. At my age my sons thought I was crazy for playing, but the joy of it was a passion that burned inside me. Speaking of which, I felt something else new, burning inside me, by just looking at this girl. Something was being rekindled. A flame that had gone out completely was beginning to be felt again. As I gazed at her when she wasn't looking, I could feel my cheeks becoming warm and flushed. They were getting hot to the touch as they do so often after making love. This was crazy, I thought. I didn't even know her name. It didn't matter. It was the eyes. I knew her eyes. And then our eyes met. I could not take mine away. I thought I must, but I could not. Suddenly she was on the bench beside me, asking me *my* dog's name. "This is Nellie," I said, surprised that any words came out at all. I think she introduced Lauren to Nellie, as only dog lovers do. Then she looked at me and said, "I'm Kay." I said, "I'm Judy." We didn't even give last names. It didn't seem important. For the moment we were just "Judy and Kay."

We hung around the table for a while longer—neither of us to this day remembers a word of the conversation. After a bit Kay got up, and I knew I must get back home as evening was drawing near and I had my dog and cats to feed, as well as a dirty, sweaty body to clean up.

It was beginning to feel really good to go home to my own little mountain house alone. I had rented such a house nestled in the cradle of an assortment of pines, hardwoods, and dogwoods, dispersed among a smattering of wild azalea, rhododendron, and mountain laurel at the foot of the Blue Ridge Mountains, not five minutes from my beloved Tea Time Farm. My little mountain house gave me a sense of both Virginia and Aspen, two different but special places that I had come to love very much. Aspen had become a spiritual place, but Virginia had somehow taken me on a journey back in time—to a place hidden in my memory of a life beyond or before. My affinity for the mountains came from deep within me, but not until I moved to Aspen and then to Virginia did it become reality. Likewise, my love of horses and the country life had always been at my core, but not until I rented the little house in the mountains of Virginia in a little town named Nellysford did I realize my heart's peace. There in that house Judy Nelson for the first time in her life was truly alone. It felt good.

But along came Kay—Kay that wonderful, dark mystery. All I could say to myself was, "It's too soon, it's too soon." I knew that Kay was to be something special in my life. I knew her. She knew me.

After Kay left the picnic table, I sat in the back of my Dodge pickup, on the open tailgate, changing my boots and putting away mallets, gloves, and knee pads. One of the guys I had played with walked up and began to chat about the day's chukkers. At that moment Kay walked up and handed me a cold beer. I don't really like beer, but it was cold and I was hot and the gesture delighted me. I almost dropped the beer for looking at her.

As the three of us spoke, the best pro in Charlottesville, my friend from Aspen Craig Ellis, joined us. He was working and teaching polo in Charlottesville during the summer before going down to where the real polo is played, Palm Beach. I asked him if he knew Kay. He didn't, so I said, "Craig, this is Kay." Then, right out of the blue, he said to her, "Are you gay?" I was mortified! I couldn't believe he had just asked this person to whom he had just been introduced such a personal question. I looked at him and said, "Craig, what a thing to ask!" He looked at me and then at Kay in utter fear and embarrassment. His face turned red and he mumbled in his Zimbabwean accent, "I didn't mean, uh, I thought, uh, well, you know, I thought you [meaning me] knew her and that maybe she was your new friend or something." He could not even look up. We all began to laugh. I explained to Craig that, no, I had just met Kay and didn't know whether she was gay or straight. Having that behind us, the two of them then launched into a discussion about South African politics. I was certain, however, that through Craig's presumption we would all know the answer to his question sooner rather than later. I had watched Kay's eyes. Despite the twinkle in them, she never answered one way or the other. I took that to mean that perhaps, just perhaps, she was. Today we laugh about it, and when we do, Craig still blushes. That is how it all began.

By now it was getting dark and everyone had gone or was beginning to leave. Kay asked the guy standing next to her if he could give her a ride home, for her sister had already left. I jumped right in on that one and asked, "How far are you going?" She said, "To my sister's, in Ivy." I knew exactly where that was and told her that it was on my way home and that I would be happy to give her a lift, if she didn't mind riding in my pickup. Kay took me up on my invitation and we two and the dogs climbed into the front seat of the truck. Rather than taking Kay to her sister's house in Ivy, I invited her to have a mocha at my house in the mountains. She had suggested a coffee in town, but I was much too dirty and tired and unpresentable to go anyplace.

After arriving at my house, I showed her around. Now it really was getting quite late. I asked her to make herself comfortable while I took a shower and cleaned up. She said she would be fine just playing with the dogs and my two special cats, Lance and Jenny. Lance, Jenny, and Nellie were my family, and I was happy that Kay and Lauren seemed to fit right in.

I tell you, as I took my shower I had no expectations about the evening other than getting to know this person whom I felt I already knew. Crazy. I know. But that's how it felt.

When I got out of the shower, I dried my hair. I left it down, falling far below my shoulders. It felt good and loose. I felt good and relaxed. I put on my oldest and most favorite pair of jeans, my softest, long-sleeved, faded-red shirt, and a touch of one of my favorite perfumes, then walked into the living room clean as a whistle and barefoot. I had the overwhelming sensation that everything felt comfortable, from my head to my bare toes. I was there. And there was Kay.

She was sitting on the large overstuffed lounge chair. I sat down on the corner of the down-filled couch. We were close enough to touch, but did not. Again, I cannot recall the conversation, for the words were not important. It was the language of our eyes that I so vividly recall. It was a language unspoken but known universally from one generation to another, from one culture to another, and from one lover to another. We moved simultaneously toward each other. We kissed—long, warm, tender, yet wonderfully passionate kisses. I held her in my arms, and she in turn held me. I could feel my heart beating against her breast and hers against mine. My cheeks were flushed and hot. I felt alive. I think my senses had been in a long, long sleep. Yes, I finally had found someone who made my heart skip a beat. My princess had kissed my lips and I had awakened.

My choice was again a woman. But this time was different. Yes, I was older, and hopefully wiser, but Kay came into my life when I was *still*. Never before had I met anyone and fallen in love when I was completely peaceful. All the passion and excitement was powerfully present, yet the feeling of calm was there, too. I would compare it to the eye-of-the-tornado phenomenon. I felt all the excitement and intensity of something being unleashed inside me, yet at my core a stillness seemed to be the source. The two forces—the passion and the calm—seemed to be in complete harmony. I knew that if I could learn to remain in that peaceful place that I could, at long last, give this woman someone whole. I knew also that I wanted that chance with her.

We were not strangers, as it might have seemed. Our souls knew each other and we trusted in that truth. From that night forward we were entwined. We shared my bed. We made end-less love. My body experienced orgasms in such quantity and with such intensity that in moments after climaxes I actually saw white light as if flashes from a camera were going off in front of my eyes. I was aware that at long last I was fully alive again, and that is why I could truly love her. I think to love a woman one must be truly alive. She demands it; she needs it; she thrives on it. I know, because so do I. Perhaps that is one of the beautiful things about loving someone of the same gen-der—when you say, "I know how you feel," you truly do.

We had not yet spoken intimately of anything. When we spoke, it seemed that the best we could do was to make feeble attempts at putting subjects, verbs, and direct objects in the proper order so as to make complete sentences and hopefully not appear to be fools in love much too soon. But we were. I knew it with every fiber of my being. Whether or not we would ever really be together was yet to be seen.

As I write this, I think of the words that the sixteenth-cen-tury French moralist Montaigne wrote when explaining why he loved his friend: "Because it was he, because it was I." I can give no greater or more heartfelt explanation than that as to why I loved Kay. I had not told her so, but I knew she could see it in my eyes, and I, too, could see it in hers.

Being with Kay is like putting on my favorite pair of old, faded jeans—something familiar, something comfortable and soft, and something I love.

The next weeks were spent in heaven. Our feet never touched the ground. We ate; we drank; we laughed; we cried. We told each other of our dreams and fears. We felt the wind on our faces as we rode our horses. We smelled the fresh, cool scent of grass beneath our bodies as we rolled on the ground, as lovers do on picnics when nobody but God is around to see. We laughed as we watched our animals run and play in the tall summer wildflowers. We lay in those flowers and we kissed and we touched. Oh, sweet love, sweet and tender love. Oh, passionate love, passionate and consuming love. The feelings are universal, my friends. Kay was my lover.

That was the way we spent our summer, a time of continuous smiles and wonderful moments of outright laughter. One particular moment, although serious at the time, now seems like a perfectly written script for a nineties sitcom episode.

Shortly after Kay and I started seeing each other and spending stolen nights and mornings together, we, like many couples, were engulfed in bliss. One evening, and then morning, wanting no distractions, I chose not to answer my phone, allowing my voice mail to record the calls. I should have checked those calls before falling asleep, for an unusual number of them came in rapid succession. I also vaguely recall the phone's ringing throughout the early-morning hours—a time when most people do not call. That should have alerted me that the people placing the calls were growing uneasy. But my desire was to stay in the wonderful moment with Kay, without interruption. I had been in New York on business and had promised to call my family when I arrived home, as had been my practice for years. I would also likewise call Michael Iott, with whom I always stayed in New York. But as I was so excited about seeing Kay again, I forgot to call anyone.

The house I had found after leaving Tea Time Farm was rather isolated with not many people close by, and my family had expressed some concern about my safety. When I didn't answer my messages, my family began to panic. My sons called my parents, my parents called my good friends the Beegles in Charlottesville. My father even called the postmaster in Nellysford the next morning. I guess Dad was hoping that someone would check on me when they delivered the mail that day. I had no idea that anyone was worried about me, but, oh, how they were.

Craig Ellis came to the rescue! Craig was living with the Beegles for the polo season. After my mother called the Beegles, they told Craig, and Craig hopped in the Beegles' old

Mercedes for the forty-minute drive out to Nellysford. I was blissfully in the arms of my lover, and she in mine. At about 10 A.M., Kay and I were peacefully sleeping, the covers pulled up around our shoulders, when suddenly we were awakened with a start by a banging on the door.

I certainly wasn't expecting anyone. We remained very still and ever so quiet, hoping whoever it was would go away. They did not. Next there was knocking at the back door. We stayed frozen in the bed, barely breathing as the knocking became insistent. I decided to have a look out the window. I rolled out of bed and crawled on the floor, keeping my head below the level of the window, and peeked over the sill. I saw a dark Mercedes, partially obstructed by the trees, parked in the driveway. At a glance it looked like Rita Mae's car. I jumped into the nearby closet—someplace I thought I would never be "in"!—and whispered to Kay, still in the bed, not to move and to pull the covers over her head. The good girl in me didn't want Rita Mae, even if we were no longer together, to see me in bed with someone. I was a bit scared because I had not seen Rita Mae since I left the farm. We had been arguing over the need for attorneys to help us separate our financial affairs. She was upset that I insisted on using them, and I was certain she had come for some verbal combat. I did not wish to confront this master of the English language who used words as her weapons as deftly as did Howard Stern or Rush Limbaugh.

The person outside came around to the bedroom window and began banging on it, obviously looking in at the very still body in the bed. I was a coward, and I don't mind telling you. Kay, by this point, was wondering *what* in the world was going on! We remained as silent as mice. Then I heard a familiar voice. I would have recognized that accent anywhere. Now, I was truly embarrassed. There I was hiding in the closet from Craig Ellis. I heard what sounded like a screen window being taken off and knew it was time to "come out of the closet." Next he would be breaking the window. I frantically put on some sweatpants and a T-shirt, ran my fingers through my hair, in comb-like fashion, went out the front door, and walked casually around to Craig, who was just about to shatter the glass. Ever so calmly, I approached him and said, "Hi, Craig. What's going on?"

From the look on his face I knew that he thought he had just seen a ghost. He said, "You're okay?!" I answered, "Of course," not realizing that I had caused so much concern over the past fifteen or so hours. I called Kay to come out (she had gotten up and dressed by then) and I said, "Craig, this is Kay. You may remember her from your introduction at the Alta Mira Polo Club." His cheeks turned red again. Now Craig knew the answer to the first question he had ever asked Kay.

Craig explained how he had seen the body in the bed and immediately thought someone had killed me. We all laughed about all the ironies before he related how worried my family and many good friends were. I called everyone and apologized, promising never to ignore my phone messages again. It was one hell of a way for everyone to find out that Kay and I were lovers, but certainly one that no one will ever forget.

After that dramatic announcement of our love affair, Kay and I spent the rest of the summer without attracting much attention. We took walks, rode horses, cooked dinners for each other, shared poetry, drove through the countryside, exchanged ideas and ideals, learned about and met each other's family. We gazed at stars and stood together on moonlit nights. And I knew once more that the joy of loving someone and having it returned has no gender. Kay was my joy.

All too soon came September. Kay was to return to her beloved France, and my future was still a big question mark. The only thing that was certain for both of us was that we loved each other. Being the romantics that we both were, we decided to try to find some way to live together. Kay decided, much to my great happiness, to go to Paris only to tie up loose ends, visit with friends, do a job for an employer whom she had promised to help, and then lease her apartment and come back to me as soon as possible. She returned in late October. In the meantime she had sent me a ticket to Paris for my birthday, so we were able to visit each other in mid-September as well. I had been to Paris many times for tennis, but that September trip was the first time I ever really saw the city. Kay knew every street and fountain and statue and museum. She knew its people, politics, food, markets, restaurants, sounds, smells, gardens, architecture, history, and wine. Kay taught me. She gave me new eyes and was teaching me to feel. Not only did she pour love into my heart, she poured knowledge into me as well. Kay was my teacher.

When she came back to me in Nellysford in October, we really began our lives together. We shared the same bed night after wonderful night. We shared the same bathroom, brushed our teeth together in the same sink. Nellysford was our home. All our animals were content and happy, and felt the security as well. Kay was my partner. Kay was my best friend.

However, I still had my insecurities. I was afraid of not being able to take care of myself, for I had only been taught how to take care of someone else. I was also afraid of being left. I had been left before. I will wrestle with that demon for as long as I live. I thought Kay would return to Paris and stay, choosing the city over me. She did not. Yet my insecurities had led me to make mistakes in the past, and they did again with Kay. But, if we are lucky, with mistakes comes forgiveness. True forgiveness binds two people together in a sacred way. Kay, too, had demons to battle. Unknowingly, often I would create situations in which her sleeping fears would be awakened, and she, like most, would want to stand and fight them.

We had danced with the angel of ecstasy and passion, and we had fought with the demon of fear and anguish. We celebrated with the angels and tried to demolish the demons. Together we stood with the hope that our love would continue to flourish and blossom, and remain strong enough to withstand any storm that blew our way. We shared fear. We shared pain. We shared hope.

It is again September. As I write this chapter, I sit at the kitchen table in Kay's tiny apartment in Paris, above a cafe in the Latin Quarter. I gaze out the window to the Place de la Contrescarpe, a cobblestone square with a lovely fountain where lovers often stroll, and students gather from the surrounding schools to laugh and eat their *pâtisserie* and sandwiches. I watch as pigeons peck at the bread crumbs dropped from the baskets of baguettes carried by the people walking in the streets. Kay and I have come to again lease her apartment, and to again celebrate my birthday. When we return, we will be embarking on an entirely new path, full of hopes and dreams.

Kay and I will move forward together following our dreams. But part of her heart will forever be in France, and part of mine will always be in the mountains. We want to find a way to realize our desires. We are both creative, energetic, and positive people, in spite of some rather difficult experiences. I think we both realize that the most important thing we can give to each other is two *whole* people. That idea is different from the one I was taught, that two people join together in order to make a whole. Kay supports me in my quests and I hope that she feels that I, too, support her in hers. It is essential. Separate and yet together. That is not a contradiction. I think it is instead the only foundation on which a solid relationship can be built. We both continue to grow. That is key. The trick is to grow in parallel directions. The destination need not always be the same, but the desire to grow must. Separation is as important as togetherness in a relationship. This I have learned. Even though Kay is younger than I, she learned those lessons at an earlier stage. She took the time to be alone. She learned the difference between being alone and being lonely. We have learned. Now, we love being just plain Kay and just plain Judy—together.

We, like most couples, will strive to make our dreams a reality. We want to find a way to spend this lifetime together as we wish, and then ours will be a union made in heaven given to us by angels. But we have learned through pain that the only thing we can know for certain is that we have today, this moment. Today Kay and I share the most passionate and intense, yet peaceful and giving, relationship that I have ever known. I know, too, that there is a delicate balance between the passion and the peace.

> Kay is my passion.
> Kay is my peace.

# 18

## Issues and Causes

Kay, my lover, has been a great source of strength when it comes to the issues and causes about which I feel strongly. She doesn't always agree with me or with my public persona, but nevertheless her insightful and sensitive interaction has challenged me to be better than I am. She has often given me the encouragement I needed to stay true to my path in the face of adversity, and to remember my values and what is of true importance in this world.

Patricia Ryan, a friend in L.A., opened the political door for me when she invited me to speak to a group of women during Lesbian Visibility Week (Patricia's vision) in West Hollywood in 1993. She prompted me to have a voice in the lesbian community and to take a stand on those gay issues that seemed important. It took a lot of courage for Patricia to invite me to speak because I was not the most popular person in the lesbian community. Many women believed I was wrong to file a lawsuit against Martina. All of that, however, led me to speak out for the right of same-sex couples to legally marry. Following are some of the issues and causes about which I have spoken or written over the past two years.*

*Many of these views on issues and causes can be found in past articles written for *L.N.* magazine, a national magazine primarily for the lesbian community.

## *Legal Marriage for Lesbians and Gays*

For some time now I have been dedicated to the lesbian and gay crusade for human rights, whether it concerns marriage and the law, discrimination in the workplace, or discrimination of any kind based on sexual orientation. Thus, I have devoted much of my time and energy speaking on behalf of the freedom for gays and lesbians to legally marry and therefore be protected by the same laws that protect all other couples in these United States. Why am I qualified to speak on this issue? Actually anyone in the gay and lesbian community is and should. I have found sometimes that experience can be the best teacher. Often that experience is painful. However, through pain we often gain insight not taught by any other means. Such was my case. My experiences as both a married heterosexual protected by the law and as a homosexual with little or no protection legally have hopefully given me firsthand knowledge as to why having equal freedoms under the law is so important to us. Had my ex-lover and I been allowed to legally marry, much of the abuse and scandal created by the media could have and would have been avoided. Had we had the right to be married under the same laws as everyone else, our disagreements could have been settled quietly and without judgment.

Our relationships should not be treated differently or with any less respect than heterosexual marriages. Homosexuals make personal and spiritual commitments to their relationships. However, because no laws protect and guide them, when a relationship breaks up, we tend to give it little or no validity. Of course, this is easy to do because society never validated it in the first place.

I also believe that when two people actually go to the courthouse and obtain a marriage license, it causes them to give serious thought to the commitment they are undertaking. Not that we don't take our private and religious ceremonies seriously, but somehow knowing that one cannot legally walk away from a relationship without some definition of the terms forces the commitment to take on an entirely new dimension.

This issue of legal marriages for lesbians and gays is not about religious ceremonies (more often than not we *can* have that these days), and it is not about trying to get any religion to endorse same-gender marriages. We, in fact, are keeping religion very separate from this issue, just as our constitution provides for the separation of church and state. This is a legal issue dealing with the liberty for all of us to enter into traditional *civil* marriages if we so choose. And with that liberty come the legal benefits and responsibilities that pertain to all legally married couples. I believe this civil freedom to legally marry will be the catalyst for all the equal freedoms that we will gain in the future. From this one act, we will take giant steps forward in our recognized same-gender relationships. By this act alone we will bypass the need for separate laws providing for domestic partnerships. That issue will simply be eliminated. Those who have attempted to gain benefits under domestic partnership laws can tell you about the thousands of dollars in legal and filing fees that they have incurred. These same benefits and more are automatically given to married couples free of charge—it simply comes with the territory.

It is important to be clear that we are asking for the *freedom to marry*—the same fundamental freedom everyone else in America enjoys except for gays and lesbians. We are not asking anything special, only equal.

In this quest for the right of gays and lesbians to marry, Lambda Legal Defense and Education Fund has been working diligently and methodically for several years on a case before the Supreme Court of Hawaii. Hopefully, it will uphold its initial decision saying that to deprive anyone of the right to marry based on sexual orientation is against the constitution of the state of Hawaii. We must be prepared for the backlash across the country that will occur if and when this happens. The radical right will be out in force, and we must, this time, be ready to do battle—not just in the courts but by all of us writing letters and making phone calls to our representatives in office, on every level, letting them know just how important this equal freedom is to us. We must continue to inform others that we are not asking for *special* privileges, but for the *same* privileges.

I am convinced that marriage is a basic human right and that this freedom will be the genesis for success in our unstoppable quest for *all* our complete and equal rights. It will be the beginning, and nothing, nothing can stop us after that. We will be able to love openly.

We, as defined in our Constitution and Bill of Rights, are a nation of people who are created equal. There should be no discrimination on any level. That is why our founding fathers came here and it is to that end that we must work. We must uphold the right to be who we are and to be equal under the law.

### Homophobia and Prejudice

One might ask, why are we discriminated against in the first place? Why do we have homophobia and how do we as a society rid ourselves of it? I do not pretend to have the answers or the cure, but because of my life experiences I can perhaps offer some helpful insights. I truly believe that we fear what we do not understand, and only through education will we reduce the fear. Through educating a society that does not understand us or even know who we are, we can lessen the homophobia that surrounds our community.

One way to educate the homophobic sector of our society is simply to put ourselves out there—let them see who we are and that we are healthy, loving, creative, and contributing people in society and that our sexual orientation is just *not* an issue.

A friend of mine, Debra Olson, said it brilliantly yet simply when she said, "We must influence, through education and exposure, those citizens who do not understand us, and therefore fear us. Segregation is as dangerous to democracy as prejudice is to the future of humanity." We must not be divided, or singled out, from the rest of society. If we continue to allow that to happen (and we often do it to ourselves, thus being our own worst enemy), then we will indeed be conquered. We must continue to create an integrated coalition of support for our community. This will ultimately assist us greatly in our united efforts to secure justice and equality for all Americans.

Speaking of equal rights, once when I was on a plane flying to San Francisco to begin a lecture series, I was sitting beside a nice-looking middle-aged woman who was apparently observing the book I was reading, *Created Equal: Why Gay Rights Matter to America* by Michael Nava and Robert Dawidoff. She leaned over and asked if she could look at it for a moment, adding that she was an AIDS activist. I gladly said yes and handed her the book. She flipped through some pages and took out a pen and paper, made some notes, and jotted down the title of the book. She thanked me. She then asked me if I was an activist, and we began to discuss some issues confronting the lesbian and gay community. As the plane landed, she turned and said to me, "You know, that book was about *equal* rights, but there is something that actually comes before that—it's about *human* rights."

I totally agreed. Yes, it is that basic. Human rights encompass all our issues. As I walked away from her to make my next connection, I knew that we had, indeed, reached out and connected with one more person. One step at a time, the process is working. Reduce the fear. Be proud of who you are, whom you love, and what you are contributing. We will change the world's perception of us, one person at a time. I do believe that.


### Lesbians and Gays "Coming Forward"

With the radical right poised to strike at gays and lesbians with every step we take forward, it would be refreshing to find a place somewhere in this world seemingly free of homophobic prejudices—a place where people could simply be themselves, no questions asked, a place where acceptance, regardless of sexual orientation, is a given, not a gift. It needs to start here.

America has always been a country where varied backgrounds and lifestyles could mesh. We need to nourish, not crush, the varied flowers in our basket. As with a gladiola, we need to allow each bud to open one by one. We must not pluck one bud from the stem because it appears different from another, for when the entire stalk is blooming, it is a sight to behold and not to be forgotten. We are all varied buds and must bloom to fill the basket.

If we as a society would learn to focus on our similarities, our philosophies, our stories of fate, our failures and successes, our ambitions and dreams, instead of focusing on what goes on in the bedroom, I think we would find that our individual sexual preferences simply do not arise as an issue. I do not think there would be an uncomfortable moment for any of us. I think we would have a healthy and happy environment that could be shared by all the world. The lesson is that there is no lesson. Why should a person's choice of a partner be something that we have to learn to accept? We need to give every human being the ability to be free and be who he or she is without pressures and prejudices. Unprejudiced acceptance is a special feeling that we should all be allowed to experience. Love is not an outward thing; peace and loving come from within, and one carries that feeling around wherever one goes.

So, I say, be who you are; feel what you feel. I believe that those special feelings between two lovers are never to be "put in someone's face"; that is not necessary. If you are happy and proud of the person you are with, it shows. The warmth and the respect between lovers can be felt. It is universal and not reserved for heterosexual couples only.

I sometimes wonder, why do we allow others or even ourselves to identify us by our sexual preferences? Whom we choose to love is not who we are, neither is it what we are. It is a part of us, but it is not our whole identity. If this is true, if each of us is capable of contributing and accomplishing, and in reality most often do contribute and accomplish, then why are we as lesbians and gays so afraid of coming forward? We must ask to be measured only by our merits—by what we give back.

*Coming forward* is a phrase I find much more positive and more descriptive than *coming out*. If you think about it *coming out* suggests that you have been *in* something, whereas *coming forward* seems to emphasize some positive movement. Perhaps we should restructure our own thoughts about how we identify ourselves and therefore reeducate a society that for the most part has negative ideas about a group of women labeled (to be kind) "different." We all know that anything that is different creates fear.

Coming forward is, in my opinion, essential for our community. We must come forward and be recognized for our achievements. We are everywhere. Why must we continue to feel that we have something to hide? We may be in the minority, but we are here.

I do know that coming forward in public can jeopardize jobs. I do know that children can undergo unrivaled peer pressure if it is known that their parents are of the same sex. However, if we do not allow the public to know who we are, how else will they ever really know us?

You may ask, as I often do, why should we have to come forward at all? Why shouldn't we just be allowed to live our lives, raise our families, make our contributions to our jobs and society without having to come forward? Why can't we just *be?* The reality is that because of our negative image, greatly due to the media's exploitation of only the rebellious, we hide in isolation. I think we must be willing to let the rest of the world know that we are as "normal" as anyone they call heterosexual.

As lesbians, we must change society's view that we either hate men or that we wish we were men. On the contrary, it is the very fact that we *are* women that we are more completely able to love another woman. If the media portrays us in any other light, then it is simply to sensationalize the unknown (and therefore boost their ratings) because we live in a world that seems to thrive on the sensational.

The reality is that we are the women next door, the women in the workplace, and the homemakers. Why then shouldn't society know and recognize who we are? We must no longer be invisible.

When I was growing up in Texas, for example, it was my recollection that there were no lesbians in Texas. We all know that in actuality there were, but believe me, they *were* invisible. I laugh and make jokes about this, but in reality I believe this to be a sad but true commentary on our position, or lack or it, in society. In our country's pledge of allegiance, we have all memorized the words "One nation, under God, indivisible, with liberty and justice for all." It does not say *invisible* with liberty and justice for *some*.

We are all role models to some young girl or woman who could perhaps have the courage to simply be herself if she realized that she was not alone—not the only one. We must be proud of ourselves, true to ourselves, and love ourselves for the people that we are. One human being truly loving another human being is something of which to be proud. Same-sex relationships can be as healthy and happy and committed as any "more acceptable" relationship in society. We are contributing forces in the workplace and in society in general, so why should we become invisible, or allow ourselves to be, when it comes to our choice of partner? In so doing we are perpetuating the "don't ask, don't tell" philosophy that we all, I think, oppose.

While reading Marianne Williamson's book *A Return to Love*, I was profoundly awakened to the fact that we, as a society, have gotten so far off track. We have somewhere been taught to focus on fear instead of love. We have lost sight of our natural tendency, our core, to focus on love. It is my belief that we, particularly lesbians, have separated ourselves from other people. We have internalized the idea that we are not quite good enough the way we are, especially because society demands that we love someone and marry someone of the opposite sex. We have learned to obey our fears and have lost our innate gentleness and hopefulness. If we are innately *loving* human beings, then how can it possibly be wrong to love anyone, no matter what the gender? It is clear to me that when life and relationships are seen from a loving perspective, then life seems to work, and it is when we look at life through our guilt and fear that we get stuck.

I have said over and over in my interviews and talks that you cannot dictate whom a person can or will fall in love with—that a healthy relationship is about two complete human beings joining together for the simple joy of loving.

I think we are all looking for that peaceful place in our lives. It is a place that comes out of loving ourselves, loving who we are, not being afraid or ashamed of who we are. Only by being still can we find that place of peace—for by being still it will come to us. This love of self can be both seen and felt—it is a certain presence, a calmness that envelops our entire being.

Step forward and be the loving, caring person that you are. And if you are judged for this, then know that you are not really the one being judged. Others are, through fear, judging themselves according to their own rules of guilt.

We used to say to be gay openly was "to be out of the closet." Now we've shortened that and refer to simply "being out." I say let's shorten even that and simply just "be." Why belittle ourselves by ever being "in" anything—especially a closet?

The best example we, the gay community, can give is to simply live our lives with pride and *be* who we are—neither trying to overpower or overwhelm our society, nor hiding our affection for the person we love in some secret closet. We should not seclude our private lives in communities and environments regarded as "only for people like us," then pretend to be someone we are not when out in society's theater. If we decide to simply *be* who we are, can it be such a threat? Will we lose jobs

Issues and Causes    183

because of it? Perhaps. But then, perhaps not. If we all were to take that risk, I dare say the world would not want to live without us. Live as though you expect to be accepted, and more often than not, you will be. Remember, we may never be completely understood by society, but we can be accepted for who we are.

## Lesbian Mothers and Their Children

Many of us have children. Many of us have to fight for the custody of them if we had them during a heterosexual relationship. Almost every woman has the choice of having them. They are forever a part of us. They are forever our children. No matter their age or ours, they are our children. How we raise them is as individual as the relationships involved.

However, we as lesbian mothers have the unusual circumstance of raising our children in a two-woman relationship rather than a traditional man-woman relationship. These circumstances are not yet well documented because little research has been published about raising children in same-sex relationships. And yet thousands of us are going about our daily tasks of raising, educating, and providing for our children.

Lesbian mothers face the question of how to raise a family when no particular structure or support system is available. Much documentation shows that all families must go through certain "stages" in their growth. However, that documentation is for the typical heterosexual family. In essence, we lesbian mothers must wing it, but we, like all mothers, can benefit by sharing our experiences with each other.

I recall watching *The Margarethe Cammermeyer Story* on TV. When she tells her sons that she is a lesbian, the youngest son replies, "You can't be a lesbian, you have children." That struck home for me. How well I remember when I fell in love with a woman, after seventeen years of marriage and two sons, and I wondered how I could possibly be a lesbian if I had children! I also thought that I was the only woman in the world this had ever happened to and that surely I was going to be a special case study for some therapist. Little did I know then that I was only one of many women who had married, had children, and later found themselves in love with another woman. I was faced with the dilemma of raising a family in an environment in which there were no known role models. The first question children usually have after the devastation of the divorce itself is, who is the "other woman?" She is not their mother nor is she their father. So, who is she? Children want to know.

In my situation, there was much confusion and anger about that issue, until our therapist helped us realize that this "other woman" was simply a friend and needed not, at that point, be anything else to my sons. With that realization, we all seemed to make some progress. No longer were they confused as to who the other woman was, and the anger began to subside. But this was not an instant fix nor was it permanent. We would slip back into old habits, and habits are hard to forget. Often I felt we would take one baby step forward and two giant steps backward. But with love and perseverance we survived, we changed, and yes, we became a family. Most of the trials and tribulations experienced in lesbian families are the same as those that the average heterosexual family goes through from day to day. But we have to go through them with some added burdens just because we are lesbians. We live in a society that declares lesbians inherently unfit mothers, giving us the message that our children somehow need to be rescued from this "abnormal" (if not immoral) situation. We are immediately faced with the dilemma that we *are* mothers and at the same time not "acceptable" as mothers. We are often confused and feel guilty, and we pass these feelings on to our children without even being aware that we are giving off such negative energy.

Regardless of what society may think, lesbians can raise healthy, happy children. We have living proof of this. I do not think that our goal as lesbian mothers is to parent identically to heterosexuals, but we need not give up all their values. We need, instead, to focus on the love that we give to our children, which is the basis of any family unit, no matter what the structure. It is through this unconditional love that we will find ways to constantly adjust to our particular situations.

## Support of the Gay Games

The Gay Games is a celebration of sport and community that has taken place every four years since 1982. The most powerful aspect of the Games, however, is not the competition itself, for you don't have to be a world-class competitor to enjoy yourself. It is instead the experience of people in relative isolation from one another coming together on a grand scale to join in the pride of their identity and in their positive contributions to society. However one participates at the Games, it is a memorable experience, from the emotional opening ceremonies to the closing ones. Often what happens off the field leaves the most lasting impressions.

I felt privileged to be in New York for the Games as one of the commentators on the TV special *Stonewall 25: Global Voices Pride and Protest* for PBS. I got an up-close-and-personal look at the Games, special events, and the community itself—an experience I had never had and one I shall never forget. There was no fear, no anger, no bitterness, and no hostility to be seen. The Games had truly achieved its high goal, that of bringing a community of special people together in harmony and unity with the freedom of being ourselves and being among a massive and positive support system.

The spirit of sport seems always to transcend boundaries. It allows us to become one in our quest for achievement, focusing everyone on our similarities rather than our differences. The Games also allows us to recognize that we are a special and sensitive group of people struggling for human rights. At the Games, I felt we were being witness to a period in history where enormous steps were being taken in that direction. One could feel that energy in New York. An overwhelming sense of change was present.

Gay Games IV was not a pageant of extravaganza or a display of polish and power and money. It was, instead, an extravaganza of heart and soul—a display of desire, determination, and pride. The Games were for everyone. No one was rejected and each participant could feel comfortable at his own level of skills.

The energy came from within, which translated outwardly into smiles and hugs and tears of joy. There was no "agony of defeat," for in every case, a higher goal had been reached and felt.

In my opinion, one of the best things about the gay community is that we don't take ourselves too seriously, that we have that wonderful ability to laugh at ourselves, while at the same time displaying courage and pride.

We are risk-takers. I hope that we all live to see the day when there is no risk in being the person one is and in loving the person of one's choice.

### Changing Partners

Changing partners in this instance does not refer to how, when, or why. Those are best left up to the couple involved and hopefully a trained counselor. It does, however, refer to how often we lesbians are perceived to be changing partners.

I draw on my personal experiences (as always) to talk about this issue, and I first want to say that I know lesbian couples who have been together for many years. But I also know that a stigma surrounds lesbian relationships concerning how many lifetime commitments we attempt to make with our various partners. This "short-term" lifetime commitment is so prevalent within our community that even *we* tend to make jokes about it. (At least we are healthy in that we can laugh at ourselves.)

So what's the point? I believe many of us profess that our innermost desire is to love and be loved and to grow old with one person. That is not to say that we necessarily want to pattern our lives after something society may have projected, but rather that the concept of loving and growing old with someone is somehow innate in all of us, whether recognized or renounced.

Therefore, what can we do to add both freshness and longevity to our relationships? We have had few lesbian role models for lasting relationships in our history because for centuries we have had to hide our sexual orientation. But the times have changed for all women, and we lesbians no longer find ourselves having to depend on our fathers or a husband for financial support, and we are coming forward by leaps and bounds. We are finally enjoying this newfound freedom in expressing our sexual preference. Often when the dust settles, we find ourselves wanting a meaningful relationship that *will* last a lifetime, and we simply don't have the right tools or the structure with which to work to create a lasting, positive, and healthy atmosphere.

How a couple attempts to stay together is as individual as the relationship, but we can all benefit by examining those relationships that seem to work and those that fall apart. We must first realize that when or if a relationship falls apart, we have not failed but have instead, hopefully, gained some new insights into ourselves and what it will ultimately take for us to enjoy and experience a lifetime commitment.

Perhaps the possibility of not committing so *quickly* would actually allow us the pleasure of dating and getting to know someone and even living with someone for a while. Much must be experienced and learned about each other beyond those early stages of bliss before a permanent commitment should be made. Jumping into a relationship at the first ringing of the bell and saying, "This is it," can be exciting and felt with every good intention, but can later prove to be emotionally and even financially hard to undo if it is not a good fit.

Talk. Talk to your lover. Talk before you and your lover make vows and promises that may prove hard to keep. Give it time, for the stages must be allowed to evolve. Be clear about your feelings, desires, hopes, and dreams. Find out who they really are and let them know, to the best of your ability, who you are before you say "I can," "I will," or "I do." Allow the relationship to go through its growing stages before asking too much of it. And then, when you are ready for a lifetime commitment, you will be much more aware of both the joys and struggles involved. And when you do make that commitment, take it seriously. It seems to me that our relationships are much too easy to get into and much too easy to walk away from. We need to give more thought and time to them in the beginning and certainly more thought and time in the end. It is often said that what attracted us to a person in the beginning is the same thing that drives us apart in the end. For instance, we fall in love with someone because she is confident and strong. Yet, that same air of confidence and display of power may in the end be intolerable. Sometimes we fall in love with someone who will take good care of us, then end the relationship by saying that we want to be independent and able to do things for ourselves. If we find qualities that attract us to someone in the beginning, then we should try not to see those qualities as faults in the end.

Yes, we all change and grow. I'm not saying that anyone should stay in a relationship that has been outgrown. What I am saying is that we should give a relationship the time and nourishment that it needs to develop. A relationship must grow *with* you, not *because* of you.

Even if you believe in love at first sight, and I certainly do, you can and should give much time and thought to creating a relationship that will last. It takes willpower and determination and a sense of devotion to stay in a relationship when in our culture it is so easy to just pack our bags and say, "I'm outta here!" I know that I enter a relationship with a lot of baggage, but I don't want to repack those bags too soon. I do want a life-time commitment.

### Family Values

I realize how fortunate I am that I can share my lifestyle with my family. I know that many in our community cannot, at least when including one's lover. Upon choosing at age thirty-eight to love and live with a woman, I remember, oh so well, that not all was perfect and harmonious when I revealed to my family and children that I was in love with a woman. As my partner-to-be was a public figure, the hope of keeping the re-lationship private was totally impossible. Therefore I was never faced with the choice of telling or not telling the decision I had made.

However, I would have told my family and friends anyway, for I cannot conceive of any other way to live. I believed that what I felt in my heart for this person was what was important, not the fact that she was someone of the same gender. The message that I expressed to my family and am still expressing to people today is, we *are* like anyone else (maybe even more special because we have gone beyond stereotypical prejudices and feel comfortable just being ourselves, not having to fit into a certain mold). We must continue to send out that message into a homophobic world as people try to pass judgment based on their experiences and values.

The most difficult part still remains: How do we tell our family and friends of our personal preferences when our choice seems so foreign to them? We do it, I continually say, one per-son at a time. We may not always have acceptance in the be-ginning, but I am convinced that in the end, understood or not, by simply being honest about our lives, *expecting* to be accepted (and looking beyond it when we are not), then eventually we will be accepted for who we are and not identified by or ostra-cized for loving the person we do.

Change is slow, however, and we must be patient. In the gay community, we all live with generations of family values that do not include our life's choices. By our example, and only by our example, can we change images and prejudices.

In my case, I found that talking with each friend or family member individually in the beginning was best. I tried meeting with the entire family at once and that was disastrous; it was like going up against an entire army totally unprepared for the force. After that failure, I decided to speak to them one-on-one, inviting them to initiate the questions. My mother's first question (and I do love her honesty for this) was, "Which one of you is the man?" And if you really think about it, that about sums it all up, doesn't it? Therein lies the problem in hetero-sexuals' thinking—that one of us in a lesbian relationship must surely play the masculine role. My reply was, "We are both women." Needless to say, there were minutes of silence. The point I made that seemed most helpful in these one-on-one discussions was that I was no different a person (my values, my styles, my mannerisms, etc.) from what I was the day before, and that their acceptance of me just for myself (not based on my sexual orientation) was crucial. Whether or not they could ever agree with or understand my choice of a same-gender re-lationship was not and could not be the issue.

The other difficult part of revealing my sexual orientation was dealing with their anger. My family, especially my children, were angry because *I* had changed their lives forever. Their paths would never be as they had envisioned. But, as in all changes, often the greatest growth is through pain. Therefore, see the pain as necessary and important.

My message is still and always will be, we are no different from anyone else. Our sexual orientation should have nothing to do with our identity as human beings and our usefulness and value within the world.

# 19

## New Careers:
## Choices at Midlife

Recently in one of my therapy sessions by phone with Annie Denver, she asked me how I had envisioned my life at fifty. I thought for a moment, then replied, "I probably always thought of myself as still being married, having grown children, lunching with my girlfriends at the club and playing a little tennis." Not so. Thankfully, I find myself with a much more fulfilling life—one with choices that both excite me and scare me to death. The main thing is that at midlife I have them.

At one time in my life I would have thought that at midlife I would be old, that the rest of my life would be downhill. The only way I could grow would be old. I don't feel old, even though a good Southern girl is programmed from birth to think of fifty as being such. I have pondered this paradox since hitting that midlife wall head-on.

Solidly believing that middle age simply means that one has acquired the rich materials of life and hopefully the means to express it, I've set myself on a course to defy the philosophy my mother spoon-fed me as her mother had to her. In past generations evidence supported the idea that at midlife a woman was old. Generations ago, living to the ripe old age of sixty-five was considered a long life. Now with all the new health, fitness, and medical discoveries, that idea has become obsolete. An entirely new frontier has been discovered.

After talks with Annie about my struggles with this paradox—that I don't feel old though I was taught to do so and fifty sounds so old—she suggested that I read Gail Sheehy's new book *New Passages*. I did. I had read her book *Passages* many times during my marriage with Ed when I was trying desperately to make some sense of my life and my marriage. What I found when I began to read *New Passages* was that the author had bumped straight into my demons. As a result she did extensive new research, providing us with a whole new life script at midlife. The most important revelation of *New Passages* is that stages that were plotted and explained in Sheehy's research some twenty years ago no longer represent the way things are. She now recognizes an age group that in the first book was merely mentioned in passing. That decade of fifty to sixty is now referred to by her as "the second adulthood in midlife." She says that women who reach the age of fifty without heart disease or cancer can expect to live to age ninety-two. So at fifty we have lived just a bit over half our lives.

With that information in mind, my thoughts of seeking a career at midlife did not seem so ridiculous. Instead they seemed both practical and exciting, and in my case both financially and emotionally essential. Sheehy's information added just the right reinforcement I needed to jump-start my battery and get started on a new adventure rather than wondering where I had spent my youth. It's funny how they say that just about the time we think we have all the answers they change the questions. I have found, like Sheehy, that the questions have indeed changed, and I am going to have to learn some new answers. I had always thought that by midlife I would have a full bag of wisdom and I could look forward to some emotional and intellectual coasting. No deal. It seems the more I've learned, the more I've learned that I haven't learned. Now that's a mouthful!

I decided the best way to embark on this new career journey at midlife was to nourish both my mind and my body. I would need both in good working order to create and perform at the highest level possible. Deciding on a fitness plan and sticking with it was essential. Luckily, I had realized that several years ago. I guess we baby boomers should give Jane Fonda some credit for that. Next, deciding on career options was important. Realizing that I *have* options at midlife is exciting. We are only as limited as our minds.

I have come to envision entry into my new decade as an opportunity for which I have longed. My children are grown, my health is good, my experiences immense, and my lessons are still being learned. With all that, I have the opportunity to follow my heart as well as my mind. I figure that at midlife I've certainly earned the right to seek to do something that I really love rather than trying desperately to love the thing that I do. I can be a risk-taker. Boy, am I scared.

However, seeing other women at my age "coming of age" gives me greater courage. Recently I had to be in New York to meet with my editor, Allan Wilson at Carol Publishing Group. While there I went with Kay and friends to see *Sunset Boulevard*, the hit Broadway musical for which Glenn Close won a Tony Award for her role as Norma Desmond (an ex–screen star, alone and in her fifties with nothing left of her life but a past that few remember and even fewer appreciate). Taking over the lead role of Norma Desmond was my childhood friend from Fort Worth, Betty Buckley, known back home as Betty Lynn Buckley. Betty, two years younger than I, gave the audience an unforgettable evening in American theater. With a well-trained but gutsy voice that supports an endless vocal range, she knocked our socks off.

Betty is a perfect example to me of what can be accomplished at midlife. In her "second adulthood" I think she must see a whole new world opening before her and is ready to establish her place in the theater as its diva. Probably if I had asked Betty at twenty, when she was a cheerleader at Texas Christian University, how she would envision her life at fifty, she would not have thought that her greatest career opportunity would have come to her at that age. Likewise, I have come to realize that at midlife I have the mind and the body and the spirit to accept the challenge and the freedom to make that choice.

The first thing I resolved to do was to write this book. I knew it would take both discipline and commitment—two really scary words! I immediately began to worry what would happen if I fell short of my goal. Would I chastise myself? Would I feel guilty? Or, if I failed, would I try to rationalize it somehow? When I recognized that I had just had all the thoughts above, I realized how far ahead of myself I was getting in my thinking. I realized once more that *my greatest lesson in life is to stay in the present, to be still.* I also remembered that through my guilt I become my own prisoner. My guilt keeps me from enjoying who I am and I became disenchanted with myself. If I allow myself to be grasped in guilt's claws if I fail (guilt being an effective teaching tool used by my parents' generation and also of generations before and after them), then my midlife journey will spiral downward until I once more hit bottom, feel the pain, dust myself off, and vow never to let the guilt surrounding failure ever take my power from me again.

I also knew that by choosing to write this book I would be taking other risks. My family might not approve because I was again subjecting them to public scrutiny because of my choices, not theirs. I was breaking a code of silence instilled in my family for generations. On the other hand, if I have something to say, and I think I do, and if my story touches lives and creates a new and better understanding between homosexuals and heterosexuals, then it is surely worth the risk. Perhaps from the choice to write this book will come other and even different career choices.

I remember learning to ride a bicycle for the first time. My daddy held the bike up and pushed it from behind as he ran along with me as I pedaled. I remember being so afraid for him to let go. I knew at some point I had to utter, "Let go," then trust that if I kept pedaling fast enough and held the handle-bars firm enough, the bike would stay balanced and continue forward. I *had* to take that risk. I think that is the same kind of lesson that I am still learning—that we always only learn the lesson by letting go, trusting and taking the risk. If I should fail, I have to pick myself up and do it again, each time with more knowledge and assurance than before.

Life will take its course regardless of how we try to manip-ulate or control it. An energy, a force, is always working in harmony with the universe, and we are happiest when we are adding to that energy—joining it, feeling it, using it. At midlife we have a whole new opportunity to do so.

We never know where or why or how our opportunities may present themselves to us. The package does not always reveal the gift. I want to open all the packages that life has put before me, for I know that the gift inside represents choices that I have if I will just look.

Not long ago I realized that the moment I began to be still—when I began to find a way into that peaceful place in-side myself—things in my life began to be more positive. Peo-ple around me began remarking at the change in me. Whatever was happening to me on the inside was showing itself on the outside. It felt good. Calls started coming in about new career opportunities. Nothing was a quick fix, but all the things were ideas worth developing. Best of all they were things I could do for myself.

A representative from the Ford Modeling Agency in New York called me after the head of their new division had seen me during a television interview. She asked if I would be interested in signing a contract with them to be a part of their Today's Woman division. I replied immediately, "That subtly means I'm over forty, right?" She laughed and said, "Yes." I signed a contract with them a couple of months later. I was flattered, but more than that I hoped for two things. One, that it would provide a new source of income. Second, that it reflected that a predominantly heterosexual society was beginning to look beyond my sexual orientation and see me for the person I am. To this date I have not had any work, so I'll scratch one and two and move on to three. I just don't know what three is.

The next opportunity that arose was a chance to do some television, only this time I would be the commentator. I was one of the anchors for a mainly gay- and lesbian-oriented show on PBS, *In the Life*, which was doing a special segment on the Gay Games in the summer of 1994. That was the beginning of what I hope will really become my new career. Radio and TV was my major in college, and at long last I was getting the opportunity to put that experience into action. After graduation from college, I had opted for the role of wife and mother and ventured into the business world only as a means of support, rather than seeking a job that I really loved. So I may be doing this "career thing" in reverse, but at least I have the experience and the knowledge and most of all the desire to do it, not to mention the need.

After doing that commentary, I wrote a column for the national magazine *L.N.* *(The Lesbian News)* about my experiences during the week of the Gay Games in New York. The editor, Katie Cotter, suggested to the publishers of *L.N.* that I stay on as a monthly columnist, writing primarily about things from my personal experiences that might be of interest to the lesbian community. I agreed. Again I was developing my own voice, and again it felt good.

From all of that exposure, and because of the faith that Judy Twersky, a wonderful PR agent in New York, has had in me, I now have other choices. I was asked to help plan two shows for two of the most popular national talk shows, segments relating to gay and lesbian issues. Both shows, I thought, helped portray the community in a positive light, as well it should be.

Hurrah for Maury Povich and Leeza Gibbons for taking a risk and helping to bridge the gap between the homosexual and heterosexual communities.

I feel the most comfortable doing television. It comes as a sort of second nature to me. If that career door opens, I'll walk right in. If it does not, then I will find another door to open. Kay and I have even formed an educational tour company, which we hope will prove to be fun and prosperous. We already have several tours, in conjunction with Virgin Atlantic Airways, scheduled to go to France. I feel a bit like the character Auntie Mame in the musical *Mame* when she sang the words from one of my favorite songs: "Open a new window, open a new door, travel a new highway that's never been tried before." Come to think of it, one of the greatest lines from that musical was when Mame identified her friend as being "somewhere between forty and death." I am somewhere between forty and life.

# 20

# Leap of Faith:
# Journey to My Soul

I'm finally learning to be still and feel the peace; it comes from within. It is a place I must go to examine my values. It is a place where I can unlock my dreams. If I cannot at the moment, then I must be patient and have faith that the day will come when I can. I think faith is what life is all about. Without it we lose life's essence. No one can ever take that away from us for we carry it in our hearts.

I think we all had faith as children. It is innate. Somehow as we got older, we learned about guilt and fear and those emotions began to consume us. I want to rid myself of those emotions as much as I can. They stifle me. They stunt my productivity. They change my perception of myself. There are always going to be changes in our lives. Sometimes I feel good about myself and sometimes I don't. What I have come to learn is that I can change how I perceive those experiences. One of my favorite sayings comes from the *Book of Runes:* "Self-change is never coerced. We are always free to resist." Change can only be realized in the present. I have been evolving all my life. I just was not as aware of it as I am now. I am finally realizing that it is not how much I go through but what I take in that matters. My leap of faith really is about just jumping into the void—about letting go of the control when I cannot have it.

To leap means to spring from one point to another. Faith means to have complete confidence or trust. Those two definitions joined together just about sum up where I am in my life right now. I'm putting on those favorite faded jeans, and my worn-out but much loved boots, with only a bunch of faith in my pockets and again heading down a new highway that's never been tried before. Where my journey will take me, I do not know. I have to take it. Perhaps it is my greatest journey of all, the journey to my soul.

I have learned that I cannot have all the answers all of the time. It is about letting go. Sometimes when I let go of those controls I love so dearly, I'm so scared that I think I won't be able to breathe. But lo and behold, I can. I find if I stay really still, not only can I breathe, but the fear goes away. It seems like such a small lesson, but it's taken me a lifetime to get it.

Now somewhere between forty (actually fifty) and life, I find myself trying desperately to rediscover the innocence I knew as a child. As children, so much of what we do is based on faith alone—no questions asked. We just do it. I think that's where I am in my life. I don't know what's out there. I just know whatever it is, I'm going to do it. I'm going to be *present*.

Thinking about the innocence of childhood, then referring to being "present," my mind goes back to sitting in the classroom as a child. I remember the teacher calling the roll to see if students were skipping school that day. When their names were called, some kids replied "Present" and some answered "Here." I thought that the kids who said "Present" were showing off. The kids who replied "Here" seemed to be more who they were without pretense. My gut feeling was always to respond "Here," but my recollection is that I sometimes responded "Present" because I thought the teacher liked it or that it seemed more polished! Oh, the good Southern girl. . . . But today I have no ambiguities. I know I want to really, really be here, no pretense. My leap of faith is about being here, wherever here is. I guess it's just a more simple way of saying I want to be *in the moment*, a more therapeutic phrase. I think I'm trying to get back to basics. Deep inside I've always known who I was and how I felt, but I've had to open a few windows, open a bunch of doors, and travel a lot of highways to become comfortable enough with my core to allow others to see me with all my flaws.

I think my leap of faith is about learning to be secure when I don't have all the answers. It is about trusting in who I am and believing in myself even when I seem to keep having to pick myself up, brush myself off, and start all over again.

As I sit in our cabin on top of this magical mountain outside the little town of Nellysford, I reflect on all my life's choices. I believe all that has happened in my life has happened for a reason. At last, I was forced to be still, to give up control. At that point and with that realization I finally began to grow.

This journey, for me, is about striving to live an ordinary life in a nonordinary way. It is about finding a way to give something back, for I have been given much. But, I also know how it feels to have everything taken away or lost, only to find that the most important things in life can never be taken away.

On the first evening I moved into our cabin on the mountaintop, I was alone. Kay had gone to Paris for a few weeks. I went onto the deck that overlooks the loveliest valley that I have ever seen. It is speckled with rolling pastures and little lakes, and trees of almost every kind and shape, providing shade and shelter for the animals in the fields. Spectacularly, I walked right out into a cloud. It came up to my knees, covering my legs and feet. I walked to the edge of the deck and looked at the valley below. It was clear. I could see the valley beneath the clouds perfectly. I was literally standing in a cloud. I had never experienced such a sensation in my life. It was breathtaking. I was overwhelmed with emotion. It was one of those spiritual moments that happens in one's life when least expected, but usually when most needed. The walk in the cloud was as moving as my revelation in the field of flowers in the mountains on my hike to Crested Butte. I related the cloud experience to a lesson that I was learning: that often we cannot see ourselves fully until we are willing to risk looking over the edge.

There is a quote I like, taken from the diary of Anaïs Nin: "And the day came when the risk to remain tight in the bud was more painful than the risk it took to blossom."

I'm ready to take the risk—to take the leap of faith. Life's journey always begins and ends with the soul.

# 21

## Just Plain Judy: My Own Voice

Yes, I have begun not only to live according to my beliefs, but to speak out about them. With my own voice I have finally begun to take control of my life, not someone else's. The words and thoughts are mine. I am no longer giving them to another. In my relationships in the past, like most good Southern women, I was willing to be the voice behind the person in my life, allowing my voice to be felt but not heard. I was a silent minority.

Looking at my choices, I believe that choosing to be with a woman is a positive choice. It is not that I have chosen not to be with a man. Men are important in my life—my daddy, my brother, and especially my sons. Men are also important to me as friends and as partners in work. I am not, nor are most women who choose to live with another woman, eliminating men from my life simply because I do not choose to have one as my husband or lover.

Shakespeare probably said it better than anyone else: "To thine own self be true." I am being true to myself, to my heart, when I follow what I feel. I never again want to live my life as someone else may feel it should be lived. I want only to live it according to my innermost feelings and desires. I want to live it with honesty, dignity, and great enthusiasm for the moment I am in.

Kay once asked me which was my favorite season. I replied, "The one I am in." (She loved that response.) That also holds true for the moment—it's the only one I know I have.

I have learned many lessons in finding myself and my voice. I have, because of my choices, been forced to examine my life and my values. I realize how much I took for granted—how easy it was to be a heterosexual in a world where lovers could openly show their affection, could hold hands or kiss without looking over a shoulder to see who might be watching. Today I find myself longing for the day when our society might perchance smile approvingly at two people in love even if they are of the same gender. The important factor would be that they are "in love," not that they are of the same sex.

The heterosexual community should keep in mind that the feelings lesbians and gays have for each other are strong. Why else would any of us endure such prejudices? My regret is that because of these prejudices so many same-sex couples have to hide their sexual orientation.

I am not ashamed, nor do I regret loving another woman. I will spend the rest of my life trying to re-educate a society that more often than not was never educated in the first place about the aspects of truly loving one's self, and therefore being able to truly love someone else, no matter what the sexual orientation. We cannot select nor tell our heart what it must feel. Feelings are not learned; they are first felt. The learning always comes after the feeling, not vice versa. Therefore, how can anyone say who we should or should not love. That privilege is as individual as the prints upon our hands.

How could I have made the choice to be with a woman so late in my life? Better still, why did I make that choice? I made it because, simply put, I fell in love with a woman. I do not feel that I need to defend what my heart felt was true and loving and beautiful. Next, how could I make that choice? The women of this century have enjoyed more sexual freedom, more economic self-sufficiency (or, are still striving for it), more education, and an ever-changing social and political climate, which have allowed them to come forward and follow their hearts. The desires to be on a more equal level and to be better understood on an intellectual level are also important to recognize. The most important factor, however, I believe is that women are becoming strong enough and self-sufficient enough to be able to make the choice to be with a woman if that is what they feel.

Having been a devoted wife and mother before becoming a lesbian taught me some important things. One, being married created a strong sense of commitment. Two, having children taught me what I had forgotten. Although I know that my choices have caused my family much pain and change beyond their control, I believe that we have all become stronger, more forgiving, more accepting people because of those choices.

I look at my mother. I know how strong and yet gentle she is—how she has and will always hold the family together. She is the hub of its wheel.

I look at my father. I know that his positive and easy manner, and his ability to recall a story and make it come alive, have held our family in an enchanted spell for all of our lives.

I look at my brother and see devotion to family and integrity and truth exemplified at their highest level. I have much respect for him.

I look at my sister. I see the real Southern Woman—one who knows the importance of family, tradition, and devotion. One who will in times of crisis be the firm hand or the soft hand, whichever is needed.

I look at Eddie and Bales, and I know there is a God and that I have been blessed. They have been my shelter in all my storms. They make my heart remember to always believe in hope and love and Christmas. They give me great joy. I did not give them life, they gave life to me.

I look at Ed. I remember young love and early marriage. That was happiness. We shared children and the joy that only that can bring. He taught me not to believe in fairy tales. He showed me understanding.

I look at Martina. She not only gave me love, but she gave me the courage to choose and to follow my heart.

I look at Rita Mae. She taught me discipline, and she challenged me to look at my core and to ask questions about it.

I look at Kay. She gives me love and teaches me about compassion. She helps me remember that "once there was a place known as Camelot" and that it does not matter if I no longer believe in fairy tales, but that I must always believe in love. I do. She gives me herself.

I look at my heritage. I am proud of my roots and of being part of three generations of a family that has always exemplified courage and given unconditional love. I have learned that because of that unconditional love I can survive almost anything. It does not necessarily make the lessons any easier or less painful, but it does help me maintain a steady course in the face of adversity and disruption.

I believe that wanting to give love and receive love is basic. It is the essence of our soul. I often wonder why any of us feels it necessary to question or judge why one person loves another. Should we not instead just celebrate with the two lovers? How easy is that? It takes so much more energy to hate and condemn. We as a society have so many more things we could be doing with our resources rather than thinking about with whom or how or why others may be sexually involved. Perhaps we should simply rejoice in the fact that they are!

Speaking of basics, when Kay and I spent several months in the cabin on top of that mountain in Virginia, we had no electricity and no phone line. We did have a generator powered by gasoline. A full tank would last only six hours or so. Temperamental, sometimes the generator started right up, and sometimes it didn't. We had to crank it up much like starting a lawn mower. When it did not start, we had to figure out why. Sometimes it was at night or it was in the rain. Sometimes it was both. We learned a lot about generators, and we learned a lot about the basic, simple way of life. We used oil-filled lanterns and lots of candles at night. We usually only ran the generator when we needed to power the computer. The generator also ran the pump that brought water from the well to the holding tank that supplied the cabin. We had cold showers; we had no showers; we had tiny trickling showers; but we learned how and when to check and fill the tank.

There were lessons learned that applied to life as well. We learned a lot of discipline. We learned never to take things for granted, such as running water and electricity to dry our hair. Television was essentially nonexistent. It taught us to be creative. When things didn't work, we had to find other ways to accomplish our goals. We were truly isolated, but we found the country folk ready to lend a helping hand for any problem. Recalling just that fills my heart with hope. No one ever seemed offended or uncomfortable that we were two women living together in the cabin. We were accepted as individuals and as a couple within the little community of Nellysford. What a great feeling.

I'm certain that the lifestyle we experienced in the cabin was much like that of a few generations back. However, we devised a way to connect a fax machine to the cellular phone and plug it all into a cigarette-lighter outlet in the cabin that was powered by a solar battery. With that modern device, we referred to our months in that little cabin as "back to the future."

I think it's time that we as a society get "back to the future"—keep all our newfound wisdom, but at the same time get back to basics. I remember calling up my daddy just a few nights after being in the cabin, the rain having not let up since we'd arrived. We were soaked, tired, and dirty. We had begun to check the oil level in the generator with fingers rather than taking the time to clean off the dipstick in the downpour. I said to Dad, "I'm going to write a book after all this and I'm going to title it *Everything My Daddy Didn't Teach Me, and Should Have!*" I guess one's never too old to learn lessons, make changes, and grow. Living with Kay in that cabin taught me that all over again in a very *real* sense.

The best part of living on the mountaintop was the wonderful and ever-changing sunrises. I have a feeling that God must be very pleased. The world is a beautiful and special place where people can experience great joy and love if they will take the time to be still. That, too, is a lesson I have learned that I hope I never forget.

I have spoken of my lessons, my life, my loves, my losses, and my lifestyle. I have spoken of them from my own perspective. I know that there will always be lessons. I know I want to embrace them and not run from them.

Now, this is *who* I am, Judy, just plain:

I love God and country and apple pie.
I love stories about Indians.
I like tepees and tents and camping out.
I love to compete.
I love to win, but can accept defeat.
I love iced tea, tomatoes off the vine, and corn on the cob.
I like Polish dill pickles.
I love long walks in country fields.
I like convertibles and stick-shift cars.
I love new Dodge Ram pickups or old Chevy ones from the fifties.
I can't sew a lick.
I do not iron.
I don't like to clean windows or put up dishes.
I like parties.

I like to dress up and look good.
I like to swim in clear, smooth ponds.
I hate to put worms on fishhooks.
I hate when I run out of tape on an answering machine.
I don't like being referred to as Martina's ex.
I crave polo.
I could eat fried green tomatoes at every meal.
I love Barbra Streisand.
I like musicals and theater.
I like Escada perfume.
I like my hair long.
I like having my teeth cleaned by Michael Iott.
I like Valentino and Donna Karan clothes.
I like to play tennis on grass without shoes.
I love Nellysford, old jeeps, and log cabins.
I love big, stone fireplaces, with roaring fires.
I like snowflakes.
I love rainbows.
I like to rock in rocking chairs.
I love clouds.
I like dried prunes and apricots.
I love hats.
I am blessed with true friends.
I love to hold babies.
I like to swim naked when no one else is around.
I like to hold my cats and rub their tummies.
I like to eat a hamburger once a year.
I like fifties and sixties music—I know the words.
I love Swiss mocha with Cool Whip on top.
I love lying in a hammock, especially with Kay.
I love poached eggs and omelettes, but I don't eat them.
I like Barbara Jordan and Anne Richards.
I don't like Pat Robertson, Ollie North, or Rush Limbaugh.
I love a good Caesar salad.

I love Bodo's Bagels.

I love to play ball with Nellie.

I love *The Sound of Music* and *On Golden Pond*.

I like the way Robert Redford, Tom Cruise, and Kevin Costner look.

I also like Vanessa Redgrave, Julie Andrews, Ava Gardner, and Candice Bergen.

I love to ride my horse like the wind with Kay on her horse beside me.

I love to see deer running.

I love the sea.

I long for the mountains.

I die for Mom's peach ice cream.

I love moonlit rides on Daddy's boat.

I could live on Mexican food from Joe T. Garcia's in Fort Worth.

I love to beat my sons at golf.

I'm addicted to Dr Pepper.

I must fax.

I love to spend weekends at Travis and Angie's camper.

I love to eat my mom's homemade pizza.

I love roasting sausages on an open fire.

I love Christmas.

I love to dance with Daddy.

I love to kiss my horse on his nose.

I like to recall stories with my mother and then laugh until I cry.

I can put lipstick on without a mirror.

I can polish my nails in the dark while riding in a taxi.

I love artichokes.

I like to learn.

I loathe prejudice.

I could eat a dozen warm, soft chocolate-chip cookies in one fell swoop.

I cherish my family.

I adore and admire my sons.

I hate to wait at red lights longer than a minute.

I still forget to fasten my seat belt.

I hate cold food that should be eaten hot.

I like to cook beans and corn bread.

I hate that money gives people power.

I love black-eyed peas on New Year's Day.

I like to pick wildflowers and put them in vases in the house.

I hate cold showers.

I love to clean my mom's mixing bowl with my finger when she has mixed the batter for a cake.

I live to give presents.

I cherish the tiny, white Bible my grandmother gave me when I graduated from high school.

I love my feather pillow.

I read Rita Dove and Maya Angelou.

I would like to see society's perception of gay and lesbian relationships change.

I crave TCBY nonfat, frozen vanilla yogurt, with sugar-free chocolate chips.

I like what Clarissa Estes said in *Women Who Run With the Wolves:* "Forgive as much as you can, forget a little, and create a lot."

I love the Blue Ridge Pig in Nellysford.

I love to go fox chasing at Oak Ridge in the fall in Virginia.

I love to make love with Kay.

I like tiny kisses on the back of my neck.

I love soft rain on my face.

I love sleigh rides.

I love long, warm passionate kisses.

I love to take walks with Kay and hold her hand.

I would like to be more spiritual more of the time.

I like old barns and fresh hay.

I love Sunday lunch at Rodes Farm Inn in Wintergreen.
I love to feel the sunshine on my face.
I like Robert Frost.
I love to light candles.
I like to talk aloud to God when I am alone.
I love old pocket watches.
I die for French green beans with garlic, lemon, and butter.
I love picnics.
I love Kay . . . and the passion and the peace.
I love my faded jeans and worn-out boots.
I like being just plain Judy.
I like having my own voice.

When I look at all these things that I love and like, as well as those that I do not, and at my lessons and my choices, I feel my life has been like a kaleidoscope. When it is shaken, it appears to be in so many diverse and fragmented pieces. However, if you look closely and adjust it ever so gently, until you get it in full focus, you find those pieces make the loveliest design. That's how I see my life. When I get the scattered pieces focused, it is a lovely design. Thank you, God, for choices.

# APPENDIX

# Documents Pertaining to My Argentine Investment

*The prospectus sent me by Dawn Wegner in December 1992
after her first trip to Argentina*

---

**FINANCIAL INVESTMENTS PRESENTED BY:**

**WEGNER FINANCIAL SERVICES**
6410 Southwest Blvd
Suite 205
Forth Worth, Texas

**A DIVISION OF DML FINANCIER**
Sarmiente 260
Lamesa Zamora, B.A.

SHORT TERM – 1 – 5 year Investments
Interest yield of up to 20% annually

---

## INTRODUCTION

Wegner Financial Investments S.A., is a continuance of
D.L.M., S.A.. D.L.M. was founded by Srs. Aldo Miret and Jose
Digiorgio over 30 years ago. D.L.M. provides financial
services for private industry and real estate on both short-
term and long-term basis.

Jorge Digiorgio has been the chief executive officer since
1978. He is a graduate of the University of Buenos Aires,
Argentina, with a bachelors degree in accounting. Sr.
Digiorgio not only has specialized in financing for the
private industry, but is also a financial advisor for the
Nacional del Desarrollo Bank in Buenos Aires.

In recent years, in the democracy of Argentina, the economy
has stabilized and is now converting over to private
industry from government owned industry. Therefore, the
demand for financing has increased.


## SERVICES

Wegner Financial Investments provides financing for the
private industry. There are three services provided. These
are:

1) Factoring of accounts receivables
2) Factoring of credit card receipts
3) Real Estate

The factoring of accounts receivables is the largest percent
of service that Wegner Financial Services offers. A company
will sell their receivables to WFI for 70 to 80% of their
value. WFI then collects 100% of the recievables when they
come due. Once 100% of the principal loan and all interest
charged is collected, then any further collections on
accounts receivables are returned to the original account
receivable owner.

Credit card factoring is also a large part of the services
offered by WFI. In Argentina, stores must wait 45 days for
payments from American Express and other large credit cards.
Most stores choose not to wait 45 days for their money and
will therefore discount these receipts to a factor for 70 to
80%. The factor then receives the full payment at the end of
45 days.

And finally, the real estate financial services are about 20
% of the total business that WFI offers. In Argentina, there

are no mortgages. What WFI offers is a loan of funds of 20% of the real estate value (based on certified appraisals). The title and ownership is then conveyed to Wegner Financial Investments. Once the principal and interest are repaid in full, title and ownership is then returned to the original owner. If the loan is defaulted, WFI sells the real estate.

All of these services offered are available on short term or long term basis and financing is available at any time. This differs from the banking industry in Argentina in that there is only short term financing thru banks and the interest rates are very high. It also takes a very long time to process loan funds thru banks, which creates a large demand for factoring.


MARKETS


The market segments that the company serves are private industry - construction, retailers, manufacturers, etc. - and local governments that need funds in the immediate future for projects.

The market area is Buenos Aires and surrounding cities, towns, and villages. There are only fifteen factors in Buenos Aires (including WFS) and out of that market WFS has a 15% share of the market.

CUSTOMERS

Business is conducted with many customers, both large and small size businesses. Some of the major clients are:

| Company | Avg Annual Business with WFS | Type of Business |
|---|---|---|
| Supermercados Camfide S.A. | $ 2,500,000 | Supermarket |
| Degrom S.A. | 1,875,000 | Steel |
| Distibuidora Santa Maria S.A. | 1,850,000 | Food Distributor |
| Electro Construcciones S.R.L. | 1,950,000 | Building Const & Electric Co. |
| Inserco del Sur S.A. | 1,700,000 | Construction - Roads, Bldgs |
| Cristaleria la Esperanza S.A. | 2,300,000 | Glass Bottle manufacturer |
| Deadoro S.A. | 1,650,000 | Food packaging manufacturer |
| Frigorifico Yaguane S.A. | 1,700,000 | Slaughterhouse |

In addition to these major clients, WFS transacts around $5,000,000 annually in the credit card factoring.

## INDUSTRY SIZE AND GROWTH

Currently, industries in all areas are growing because of changes is the economic conditions in Argentina, as well as the political changes that occured during the 6 year term of President Menen.

With the derregulation of certain industries and the opening of new businesses now allowed, the need for financing is growing at a tremendous rate. The demand is increasing ten fold therefore creating a need for existing factors to have funds available to finance this growth.

In the last three years, under President Menen, the inflation rate has dropped 40% and has now stabilized at 18%. The dollar and peso are now valued at the same rate of exchange, there is no welfare in Argentina, and there is socialized medicine. This has created a ripe environment for businesses.

WFI (formerly DML) has a proven record of 30 years in business to show that it is recession proof.

## BUSINESS STRATEGY

Wegner Financial Investments is currently pursuing a larger market share. Their objective is to increase the volume and share faster than competition and faster than the general industry growth rate.

To pursue this line of strategy, the focus will be on the new markets created by economic prosperity in the environment. The objective is to capture a larger share of the market growth.

In order to achieve these objectives, external financing is required in order to increase internal investment to speed the growth of the business.

INVESTMENT

Because of the great economic prosperity occuring, external
financing is being pursued for the factoring of accounts
receivables on a short term basis.

## Investments under $100,000

You, the investor, purchases a certificate of deposit for
the time period, i.e. 2 year earning of interest is a 24
month CD. The CD is purchased in your name. The CD is
transferred to a New York-Argentina Bank and held as
collateral, for which you will be properly receipted.

At the end of the time, the CD will be returned to you,
along with the interest check.

Example, your CD earns 4% - Wegner Financial Investments
agrees to pay you an additional 16% which totals 20% annual
interest on a 2 year investment.

## Investments over $100,000

You, the investor, purchase U.S. Treasury Bills. The TBills
are purchased in your name. The TBills are transferred to a
New York-Argentina Bank and held as collateral, for which
you will be properly receipted.

At the end of the time, the TBill will be returned to you,
along with the interest check.

Example, your TBill earns 8% - Wegner Financial Investments
agrees to pay you an additional 12% which totals 20% annual
interest on your investment.

For larger sums of money, your bank will purchase
"repurchase agreements" of U.S. Government paper to be held
by a U.S. bank as custodian. This paper will then be pledged
as collateral, the same as the Certificates of Deposits.

The time period for these transactions will vary between no
less than 1 year or greater than 5 years.

*Letter from my U.S. attorney to my Argentine law firm to work out*
*options in pursuing my case against Jorge DiGiorgio*

KIRKLEY SCHMIDT & COTTEN, L.L.P.
*Attorneys at Law*

DAVID BROILES
DENNIS M. CONRAD
LARRY I. COTTEN
BRIAN D. ESENWEIN
STEVEN K. HAYES
J. LYNDELL KIRKLEY
DAVID A. LOWRANCE
JOHN D. MIXON
RANDALL SCHMIDT

2700 CITY CENTER II
301 COMMERCE STREET
FORT WORTH, TEXAS 76102-4127

CHRISTOPHER BULEY
STEVEN J. GORDON
PAUL E. HANSON
S. JAN TURNER

TELEPHONE:
(817) 338-4500

FACSIMILE:
(817) 338-4599

January 13, 1994

<u>VIA FACSIMILE TRANSMISSION</u>

Mr. Dámaso A. Pardo
Mr. Juan Murga
Mr. Ignacio Randle

1309 Buenos Aires
República, Argentina
(54-1) 372-6619

RE:    Judy Hill Nelson v. Jorge DiGiorgio

Gentlemen:

Following my discussion with your office on December 14, 1993, Judy Hill Nelson and I met with Jorge DiGiorgio in Fort Worth, Texas on December 27, 1993. Mr. DiGiorgio proposed delivering to Judy Hill Nelson the sum of $XX,XXX (U.S.) cash without signing any documents.   During the course of the discussion and negotiations that occurred on December 27, 1993, I obtained a document which contained the words that he was handling her investment on an "administration basis" as recommended by your office.  I enclose a copy of the document signed by Jorge DiGiorgio and Judy Nelson on December 27, 1993 which states:

> I, Jorge DiGiorgio, a citizen of Argentina have this date paid to Judy Nelson the sum of $XX,XXX (U.S.) cash as part payment of the $XXX,XXXxx (U.S.) investment that I have administration on for Judy Nelson with transfer to me by Judy Nelson wired to Citibank Account #XXXXXXX-XX on 28 October 1992.

I believe that this document complies with your advice that he sign a document stating that he has administration of funds that were previously transferred to him for possible criminal action.

Mr. DiGiorgio has promised that he will make another payment on these monies administered by her in February 1994 approximating $XX,XXX.  Before instituting any criminal proceedings, we would like to know the following:

*219*

Mr. Dámaso A. Pardo
Mr. Juan Murga
Mr. Ignacio Randle
January 13, 1994
Page 2

(1)    Is this document sufficient to show that he is administering funds for Judy Nelson and has breached various agreements and representations concerning repayment of monies to her which he promised to pay in November 1993?

(2)    Is there any civil action that can be brought against Mr. DiGiorgio based on this document and the other documents?

(3)    If this gives rise to a criminal action based on the enclosed document, what would the charges be for handling such criminal action against Mr. DiGiorgio if he fails to make the payment in February 1994?

Please correspondence with respect to these questions by letter to me at fax number (817) 338-4599.

Best regards.

Yours very truly,

Original Signed by
J. LYNDELL KIRKLEY

J. Lyndell Kirkley

JLK:lld
Enclosure

cc:    Ms. Judy Nelson

*Two letters from Pablo Richards, my Argentine attorney.*
*The gist indicates the futility of my case.*

Enrique Abeledo (1925-1980)
allo Gottheil
sé M.García Cozzi
uis A.Erize
ntonio Avila
blo A.Pinnel
arcelo E. Gallo
rge E. Tützer
an Pablo M.Cardinal
driana M.Schapira
uis Matías Ponferrada
alixto Miguel Zabala
dro F. Tami
a Narvarte
dro E. Arieu
vier L. Magnasco
lio A. Viello
abriela I. Buratti
blo F. Richards
ago Daniel Corazzini
resa E. Anders
vina G. Goldenberg
aría S. Nuviala
rina Monvro
aría F. Maggi

nsultor:
rge E. Rivarola

ludio Asociado:
, Andrés Badessich

ABELEDO GOTTHEIL ABOGADOS

GOTTHEIL-GARCIA COZZI-ERIZE

AV. E. MADERO 1020 - PISO 5
1106 BUENOS AIRES
ARGENTINA
1?

Tel. 312-7526/7527/7528
312-7529/7520/4058
315-4721/4722/4723
313-0825/1671
311-3560
315-4068

Telefax: 312-7526/7527/7528
312-7529/7520/4058
315-4721/4722/4723
313-0825/1671
311-3560
315-4068

Buenos Aires, July 6, 1994

Ms. Judy Nelson

Dear Judy:

We met yesterday with Mr. Oscar Meola, partner of Mr. Jorge Digiorgio. Although we collected only promises, it seems that they are prepared to talk on reasonable terms on the redelivery of the monies received.

(i)    First of all Mr. Meola said that as soon as Digiorgio received your remittance in October 1993 he in turn delivered to Mr. Frank Albero u$s XXXXXX without executing any contract or giving instructions; he only has a receipt that Mr. Meola promised to produce next meeting.

Obviously we argued that in all cases they must search the recovery of the money plus agreed interest to, in turn, delivery it to you.

Mr. Meola requested us a waiting period of around 72 hours to contact Frank Albero and arrange how they are going to recover the money.

(ii)    Mr. Meola indicated that the u$s XXXXXX was lended jointly to Cristaleria de Cuyo and Cristalería Esperanza (u$s XXXXX) and to a company called Degron (u$s XXXXX). Both have financing problems but the Cristalerías will, during next week, pay back the capital plus the agreed interest.

1

mbro del South American Business Law Group

Abeledo Gottheil Abogados
theil-García Cozzi-Erize
nos Aires
entina

Baptista,Carvalho Tess
& Hesketh
Sao Paulo
Brasil

Paraco de Azevedo
Porto Alegre
Brasil

Estudio Jurídico Otero
Santiago
Chile

Estudio Jurídico
Jiménez de Aréchaga
& Brause
Montevideo
Uruguay

According to Mr. Meola this will enable them to pay back to you the u$s xxxxxx retained by Digiorgio and Meola plus the interests on that amount for all the period since the amount was received until payment.

Finally Meola promised to send today (up to now we did not receive it) a summary of the outstanding debt plus interests updated.

As you may see, the received promises are encouraging but we will have to wait until we can go down to facts to see if Messrs. Digiorgio and Meola have a real will to pay back the amounts they received from you plus interests, and if such will is backed up by a guaranty or a real possibility of obtaining the necessary funds.

We will revert as soon as any further news are available.

Best regards,

Pablo F. Richards

Enrique Abeledo (1925-1980)
lio Gottheil
é M.García Cozzi
ls A.Brize
ntonio Avila
blo A.Pinnel
arcelo E. Gallo
rge E. Tützer
an Pablo M.Cardinal
dro F. Tami
riana M.Schapira
is Matías Ponferrada
lixto Miguel Zabala
a Narvarte
dro E. Arieu
er L. Magnasco
io A. Vieito
abriela I. Buratti
blo F. Richards
ugo Daniel Corazzini
rosa R. Anders
vina G. Goldenberg
aría S. Nuviala
rina Moavro
aría F. Maggi

nsultor:
rge E. Rivarola

tudio Asociado:
res. Andrés Badessich
is Basavilbaso

# ABELEDO GOTTHEIL ABOGADOS

## GOTTHEIL-GARCIA COZZI-ERIZE

AV. E. MADERO 1020 - PISO 5
1106 BUENOS AIRES
ARGENTINA

Tel: (541) 312-7526;  (541) 315-4721

Fax: (541) 312-4058;  (541) 311-3560

Miembros del South American
Business Law Group:

Abeledo Gottheil Abogados
Gottheil-García Cozzi-Erize
Buenos Aires
Argentina

Baptista, Carvalho Toss & Hosketh
Sao Paulo
Brasil

Furaco de Azevedo
Porto Alegre
Brasil

Estudio Jurídico Otero
Santiago
Chile

Estudio Jurídico
Jiménez de Aréchaga & Brause
Montevideo
Uruguay

Buenos Aires, October 24, 1994

Ms. Judy Nelson
Net Results Ltd.
U.S.A.

Dear Judy:

The letter was delivered to an employee who received it on behalf of Mr. Jorge Daniel Digiorgio on October 15, 1994.

We have not been contacted through the telephone nor we received any written answer, although the granted five day limit expired on Friday last.

It seems that this type of pressure will have no effect on Digiorgio. Perhaps it is time to use your contact with the American Embassy in Argentina.

I think that the service they may be able to render at the beginning is to summon Mr. Digiorgio to the Embassy where they could let him know that an agreement to settle this claim will be very well received.

I look forward to receive your comments.

Best regards,

Pablo F. Richards

AMERICAN EMBASSY, BUENOS AIRES, ARGENTINA

ECONOMIC SECTION

FAX MESSAGE

-------------------------------------------------------------------------------

Date:    December 1, 1994

From:    Peter D. Whitney, Economic Counselor

FAX:     (541) 777-0197   Phone: (541) 777-1584

-------------------------------------------------------------------------------

We have reviewed the documents you sent me regarding the
DiGiorgio case.  We found out that:

-- We could not reach Jorge DiGiorgio.  In his proposal to Ms.
   Nelson he did not use letterhead paper and he is not listed
   in the Buenos Aires telephone directory.  Nevertheless, we
   would guess he would not reply to any call regarding the
   subject;
-- His company, DLM Financer, is not known in the financial
   markets;
-- Out of the eighth companies listed by Mr. DiGiorgio, three
   are not known at the business community and not listed in
   the Embassy's Commercial Section reference books;
-- One of the companies listed, Frigorifico Yaguane, has
   allegadly a legal problem for using fake forms to export
   meat under the Hilton quota.  According to press reports,
   the case against Frigorifico Yaguane was softened after the
   owner and former Minister of the Interior Mera Figueroa
   talked to his political allies.  Clippings dated Oct. 20,
   1994 describe the actions taken recently in favor of
   Yaguane;
-- Ms. Nelson's legal representatives in Buenos Aires are well
   known and respected;
-- As you understand, this is a private case which the
   partners involved will have to resolve.  The Embassy can do
   very little or nothing.

I hope what we were able to do may be of help.

*Peter*

29 March 1995

Senator Kay Bailey Hutchison
283 Russell Senate Office Building
Washington D.C.  20510

Dear Kay,

Today we hear a lot of discussion about abuse of women in the workplace. Most often we are speaking of <u>sexual</u> abuse. I'm writing you because I believe there is another kind of abuse of women that never makes the headlines--that of <u>financial</u> abuse. This kind of abuse stems from the vulnerability, and to a great degree, the innocence of women. I am victim of financial abuse.

In this letter I will explain my case, and the documents enclosed herein will provide a "paper trail" of the tragic ordeal. Before I begin my story I want to tell you that I have been attempting in every possible way to retrieve my investment. It has been since November 24th, 1993 that my investment plus interest was due, and to this date after incurring thousands of dollars in attorneys' fees I have only been able to retrieve $XX,XXX.xx of my life's savings of approximately $XXX,XXX.xx. I invested exactly $XXX,XXX.xx. in Argentina on November 24th, 1992 for one year with a guaranteed percentage of 24%--the principle plus interest to be paid in full to me on November 24th, 1993. It was not.

Over the past year and a half not a day has gone by that I have not thought about or delt with the problem in some way. I awoke just the other morning with the realization that up to this point I had only delt with men and I <u>knew</u> that I needed to tell my story to a woman, for perhaps only a woman would fully understand my dilemma withoiut seeing it as simply a huge mistake.

Being born in Fort Worth, Texas (as were my parents, their parents having travelled to Texas in covered wagons), and having lived there all my life and raised my two sons there, I thought the best thing to do would be to write a letter to you, one of the most powerful and influential women in Texas, as well as my U.S. senator.

I do believe that had I been a man I would never have been taken advantage of in this way in the first place. I also believe that had I been a man the attorneys and government officials that I have delt with thus far would have been much more agressive in uncovering and exposing this "con job." What has occurred is an injustice and, I'm certain, has and will happen to other women unless we confront the issues involved and win.

In 1992 I was in a very vulnerable state of mind, having lost a committed relationship of nearly eight years. I was a woman, alone, and in mid-life faced, perhaps for the first time in my life, having to make a financial decision on my own. I had received a house in the previous relationship. I sold it and wanted to invest most of that money in a way that would create enought income that I could live on the interest earned and save the principle. I still had two sons in college, both wanting to go on to graduate schools. I had always shared equally in their support and education since my divorce form their father ten years prior. At the time I was 47 years old and I had to consider how I would support myself for the rest of my life as well as educate my sons.

A friend and former business partner, Frank Albero, came to me and suggested that he help me with my finances. I trusted him. I was vulnerable and innocent, and I believed that he truly wanted to help me create a secure future for myself and my sons. He advised me to invest my money in Argentina. He told me of his business partner in Buenos Aires who had what he called a "factoring company." He explained that term to me and said that my money would be safe and that I could live on the 24% that would be a guaranteed interest on my money. The agreement that I signed (documents enclosed) was for one year and after that I could choose to renew the agreement or not. When the year was over and the investment plus interest was due I was told many "stories" but none of them produced my investment. I began to panic. I made calls every day. Finally, the two men, Frank Albero and his partner in Argentina, Jorge Di Giorgio, agreed to meet me in New York. I was to receive "some of the money." I did not. I did, however, get Di Giorgio to sign a paper saying he indeed owed me the money, as my Argentina attorneys had advised.

Another meeting was agreed upon the next week in Texas with my Texas attorney present. I received $XX,XXX.xx after an entire day's discussion about the real whereabouts of my investment. Di Giorgio, at the insistence of my Texas attorney signed another note verifying the fact that he owed me the balance due from my initial investment and its accrued interest. He made a phone call which my attorney and I listened to his "other partner" in Buenos Aires guaranteeing that another $XX,XXX.xx would be sent to me within the next month. It was not.

You will read in the letters and faxes enclosed the actions that were taken and the transactions that have taken place since that meeting in Fort Worth, Texas.

I have been advised by my attorneys in Buenos Aires that my only recourse (because Mr. Di Giorgio feels no real pressure from me) at this point is to file criminal charges which could take as long as five years to come before the courts and be entirely too costly (since I now have no money at all now) and if I were to win, he would be put in prison, but I would not receive any of my money. That is not an option.

My Argentina attorneys then advised that I try to get the American Embassy to help by putting pressure on him by suggesting that they would revoke his passport to the U.S.

My attorneys spoke with an official at the U.S. Embassy who suggested that they would help only if they received some official word or support from a government official in the U.S.

That brings us to this moment and this letter. I need your help. I know that I am just a single woman and that our government has many more important issues with which to deal. But I am one of those "we the people" and I need some help from my government "of the people."

I need to believe that a single woman and mother can be heard and helped. Will you help me? I need only a letter of support or a phone call to the U.S. Embassy in Buenos Aires. I thank you for the consideration.

With respect,

Judy E. Nelson

KAY BAILEY HUTCHISON
TEXAS

## 𝔘nited 𝔖tates 𝔖enate

WASHINGTON, DC 20510–4304

April 24, 1995

Mrs. Judy E. Nelson
4 Shingle Oak Lane
Nellysford, Virginia 22958

Dear Mrs. Nelson:

Thank you for your follow-up letter of March 29, 1995. As you have probably already know, foreign investments are not protected by our government. I will, however, be happy to forward you concerns to Ambassador Cheek in Buenos Aires. Your complaint against Frank Albero and Jorge Di Giorgio will be made a part of the official records of the U.S. Embassy in Argentina. Additionally, I have provided this information to the ^U.S. Department of State in Washington, DC.

A complaint is not sufficient to preclude the issuance of requested travel documents. Should civil or criminal charges be filed against these individuals and the Courts find them guilty as charged, then of course, their passports would be suspended.

I realize this is no consolation to you, since your life savings are involved, but schemes such as you've experienced are fairly common. When inquiries are made to the Department of State prior to making an investment they are advised that these are risky as best and most often totally unreliable.

I wish you success in your efforts to recover your investment.

Sincerely,

Kay Bailey Hutchison

KAY BAILEY HUTCHISON
TEXAS

COMMITTEES:
ARMED SERVICES
SMALL BUSINESS
COMMERCE, SCIENCE,
AND TRANSPORTATION

# United States Senate

WASHINGTON, DC 20510-4304

June 1, 1995

Ms. Judy E. Nelson
4 Shingle Oak Lane
Nellysford, Virginia  22958

Dear Ms. Nelson:

Please find enclosed for your review an interim response I received on your behalf from the Department of State.

I am awaiting additional responses and will contact you again as soon as I receive a reply. In the meantime, should you have any questions, please feel free to contact my staff assistant, Mary Fae, in my Dallas office.

Sincerely,

KAY BAILEY HUTCHISON
United States Senate

KBH/mfk
Enclosure

IIIIIIIIIIIIIIIIIIIIIIII
UNCLASSIFIED

ACTION

*Department of State*

PAGE 01    BUENOS  95 5 MAY 5 031932Z PH 1: 35                SHC5005
ACTION HCRE-01

INFO  LOG-00    ARA-00    COME-00   OASY-00   EB-00    FBIE-00   H-01
      TEDE-00   ADS-00    TRSE-00   /004W
      ------------------C1DAEC   031932Z /38
P 032028Z MAY 95
FM AMEMBASSY BUENOS AIRES
TO SECSTATE WASHDC PRIORITY 5768

UNCLAS BUENOS AIRES 002565

H PASS

E. O. 12356:  N/A
TAGS:  EFIN, AR
SUBJECT:   CONGRESSIONAL CORRESPONDENCE

TO: HONORABLE KAY BAILEY HUTCHISON
UNITED STATES SENATE
DALLAS DISTRICT OFFICE
10440 N. CENTRAL EXPRESSWAY
SUITE 1160, LB 606
DALLAS, TX  75231

ATTN:  MARY FAE KAMM, DIRECTOR, CONSTITUENT SERVICES

DEAR SENATOR HUTCHISON:

THIS IS IN RESPONSE TO YOUR LETTER OF APRIL 19
CONCERNING THE FINANCIAL DISPUTE BETWEEN JUDY E.  NELSON,
                                              AND
COMPANIES IN ARGENTINA.

THE EMBASSY FINANCIAL OFFICER, PATRICK SYRING, WILL
CONTACT YOUR OFFICE AND WILL CONTACT MS. NELSON'S
ARGENTINE ATTORNEY ABOUT HER CASE.

PLEASE DO NOT HESITATE TO CONTACT US AGAIN SHOULD YOU
BELIEVE WE COULD BE OF ASSISTANCE.

SINCERELY,


JAMES R. CHEEK
AMBASSADOR
CHEEK

H
P
A
S
S

UNCLASSIFIED

Buenos Aires,
May 8, 1995


Mr. Jorge di Giorgio
Sarmiento 260
1832 Lomas de Zamora
Provincia de Buenos Aires


Mr. di Giorgio:

Senator Hutchison of Texas has brought to our
attention the financial claim which Judy E. Nelson has
against you.

You are advised to make arrangements to repay Mrs.
Nelson. Otherwise, she would be in a position to seek a
criminal judgement which could prohibit your entry into
the United States as a felon.



Patrick Syring
Financial Officer
U.S. Embassy
Buenos Aires

*Letter to me on July 7, 1995, from the U.S. Embassy Finance Office in Buenos Aires suggesting that there was nothing further its staff could do . . . I would have to pursue the case at my own expense.*

Embassy of the United States of America

Buenos Aires
July 7, 1995

Ms. Judy Nelson
4 Shingle Oak Lane
Nellysford, VA   22958

Dear Ms. Nelson:

This is in reply to your letter of July 6 concerning your dispute in Argentina.  A certified letter was sent May 12, 1995, to
    Jorge Di Giorgio
    Sarmiento 260
    1832 Lomas de Zamora
    Provincia de Buenos Aires

Mr. Di Giorgio has not been in touch with us so far, and we are unable to confirm if he received the letter.  Foreign Service Officers are prohibited from serving documents personally.  I urge you and your attorney to contact Mr. di Giorgio directly.

If you wish to hire another attorney, I am enclosing a list of private attorneys registered with us for your possible use to act on your behalf.  Although the list was prepared with care, we cannot assume responsibility for the personal integrity or professional ability of the attorneys listed.

Patrick Syring
Finance Officer